P9-CFT-818

11/05

WILLIAMS-SONOMA

CHRISTMAS

RECIPES AND TEXT
CAROLYN MILLER

GENERAL EDITOR
CHUCK WILLIAMS

PHOTOGRAPHS
MAREN CARUSO

SIMON & SCHUSTER • **SOURCE**

NEW YORK • LONDON • TORONTO • SYDNEY • SINGAPORE

CONTENTS

SOUPS AND SALADS

THE MAIN COURSE

SIDE DISHES

DESSERTS

HOLIDAY BREAKFAST

OPEN HOUSE

INTRODUCTION

Every year, we enjoy celebrating the many holidays each season brings, but Christmas has become more than a holiday. It has become an important focal point of entertaining that we anticipate as each year ends. This collection of recipes will help you organize all of your entertaining, whether it is a traditional Christmas dinner, a winter supper with friends, a Hanukkah celebration, a welcoming open house for colleagues, or a festive New Year's Eve party. I am sure you will find just the right combination of recipes in these pages for any entertaining ideas you have—whether you are searching for a comforting soup, an unforgettable roast, or an elegant dessert.

At the back of this book, you will find a chapter titled "Christmas Basics" that gives in detail all you need to know to make your holiday entertaining easier, and I encourage you to read this section before you begin planning any celebration. This is a book you will turn to year after year to help you with your Christmas entertaining!

Chuck Williams

SOUPS AND SALADS

A warming, luxurious soup is an inviting and elegant opening for any holiday meal—as is a salad of winter greens, bright with the season's crisp fruits and vegetables. These starters make a festive prelude to the feast that follows.

CRAB BISQUE

In a large soup pot, melt the butter with the oil over medium heat. Add the shallots and sauté until translucent, 2–3 minutes.

Add the stock and cream to the pot and season with kosher salt and white pepper to taste. Bring to a simmer.

Reduce the heat to low and stir in the crabmeat. Cook until heated through, about 5 minutes. Stir in the sherry and heat for 2–3 minutes. Taste and adjust the seasoning.

Ladle the soup into warmed shallow bowls and garnish with tarragon. Serve at once.

MAKES 8 SERVINGS

CRABMEAT

The best-tasting crabmeat comes from crabs you cook yourself. If you have access to live crabs, use them to make bisque. Two 2-lb (1-kg) Dungeness crabs or eight to ten hard-shelled blue crabs will yield about 1 lb (500 g) of crabmeat. You can also buy cooked crabs and extract the meat. Fresh lump crab-meat is the next-best option, especially if you are short on time; look for it at fish markets. Otherwise, use frozen or canned crabmeat, drained and quickly rinsed.

1 tablespoon unsalted butter

1 tablespoon canola or grapeseed oil

3 large shallots, minced

5 cups (40 fl oz/1.25 l) fish stock, chicken stock (page 117), or prepared low-sodium chicken broth

2 cups (16 fl oz/500 ml) heavy (double) cream

Kosher salt and freshly ground white pepper

¾–1 lb (375–500 g) fresh or thawed frozen lump crab-meat, picked over for shell fragments (about 3–4 cups)

½ cup (4 fl oz/125 ml) dry sherry, dry Marsala, or Madeira

Minced fresh tarragon or flat-leaf (Italian) parsley for garnish

CREAM OF MUSHROOM SOUP TOPPED WITH PUFF PASTRY

FOR THE PUFF PASTRY TOPS:

2 sheets thawed frozen puff pastry

1 large egg

1 tablespoon milk

8 cups (64 fl oz/2 l) chicken stock (page 117) or prepared low-sodium chicken broth

6 tablespoons (3 oz/90 g) unsalted butter

3 tablespoons olive oil

3 shallots, minced

3 tablespoons all-purpose (plain) flour

1½ lb (750 g) mixed fresh mushrooms such as cremini, porcini (ceps), portobellos, and chanterelles, brushed clean and coarsely chopped

Kosher salt and freshly ground white pepper

⅓ cup (3 fl oz/80 ml) dry Marsala or brandy

1 cup (8 fl oz/250 ml) half-and-half (half cream)

2 tablespoons minced fresh chives

To make the puff pastry tops, preheat the oven to 400°F (200°C). Line 2 baking sheets with parchment (baking) paper.

On a lightly floured surface, roll out a sheet of puff pastry to a thickness of about ⅛ inch (3 mm). Cut out 4 or 5 rounds slightly smaller than the top of the soup bowls you will be using. Place the rounds on one of the prepared pans. Repeat with the second sheet of pastry. In a small bowl, using a fork, beat the egg with the milk. Using a pastry brush, brush the rounds with the egg mixture. Bake until golden brown and puffed, about 15 minutes. Transfer the rounds to a wire rack and let cool.

In a large saucepan over medium-high heat, bring the stock to a rapid simmer. Meanwhile, in a large soup pot, melt the butter with the oil over medium heat. Add the shallots and sauté until translucent, 2–3 minutes. Stir in the flour and cook, stirring constantly, for about 3 minutes; do not let the mixture turn brown. Stir in the mushrooms and season with kosher salt and white pepper. Cook, stirring occasionally, for about 3 minutes. Remove from the heat and whisk in the simmering stock. Return to medium-low heat, cover partially, and simmer gently until the mushrooms are tender and the soup is flavorful, 20–25 minutes. Remove from the heat.

In a blender or food processor, purée the soup in batches until smooth. Return the soup to the pot, place over low heat, and bring to a simmer. Stir in the Marsala and simmer for about 3 minutes. Stir in the half-and-half and simmer for about 5 minutes. Taste and adjust the seasoning. Remove from the heat.

Stir in the chives and ladle the soup into warmed shallow bowls. Top each bowl with a puff pastry round and serve at once.

MAKES 8–10 SERVINGS

PUFF PASTRY

One of the glories of French cuisine, puff pastry is made by adding layers of butter to pastry dough through repeated rollings and foldings, producing a rich, flaky dough used in savory and sweet dishes. Frozen puff pastry dough is a fine substitute for labor-intensive homemade. It will be ready to use at a moment's notice for hors d'oeuvres, main dishes, and desserts—or to crown flavorful soups like this one. Defrost the dough in the refrigerator according to the package instructions, and keep chilled until ready to use.

BUTTERNUT SQUASH AND APPLE SOUP

In a large soup pot, melt the butter with the oil over medium heat. Add the shallots, ginger, cardamom, and cumin and sauté until the shallots are translucent, 2–3 minutes. Add the squash and apples and sauté, stirring frequently, until they begin to soften, 2–3 minutes. Add the stock and season with kosher salt and white pepper to taste. Raise the heat to high and bring to a boil. Reduce the heat to medium-low, cover, and simmer until the squash and apples are very tender, about 40 minutes.

In a blender or food processor, purée the soup in batches until very smooth. Return the soup to the saucepan and reheat over medium-low heat. Add the lemon juice and cayenne. Taste and adjust the seasoning.

Ladle the soup into warmed shallow bowls. Garnish with a swirl of thinned crème fraîche and a sprinkle of chives.

Note: To use crème fraîche as a garnish for this or other puréed soups, thin it first with milk until it reaches a pourable consistency.

MAKES 8-10 SERVINGS

BUTTERNUT SQUASH

Although any winter squash—such as acorn, kabocha, or delicata—could be used for this fragrant soup, butternut is the meatiest and one of the most flavorful of all hard squashes. Its long, bulbous shape and pale beige color are unmistakable in the market, while its size makes it easy to prepare for soups and purées: Using a large chef's knife, cut the squash in half lengthwise. Remove the seeds and strings from the cavity, then carefully cut off the skin with a small, sharp knife. Chop the squash as directed in the recipe.

1 tablespoon unsalted butter

1 tablespoon canola or grapeseed oil

3 shallots, minced

1 tablespoon peeled and minced fresh ginger

1 teaspoon ground cardamom

½ teaspoon ground cumin

1 large butternut squash, about 4 lb (2 kg), peeled, seeded, and coarsely chopped (*far left*)

3 large tart green apples such as Granny Smith or pippin, peeled, cored, and coarsely chopped

6 cups (48 fl oz/1.5 l) chicken stock (page 117) or prepared low-sodium chicken broth

Kosher salt and freshly ground white pepper

2 teaspoons fresh lemon juice, or to taste

Pinch of cayenne pepper

Crème fraîche (page 121), thinned with milk (see Note) for garnish

Minced fresh chives for garnish

OYSTER STEW WITH FRESH ROSEMARY

1 tablespoon unsalted
butter

1 tablespoon canola or
grapeseed oil

1 small yellow onion, finely
chopped

2 celery stalks, finely
chopped

¼ cup (2 fl oz/60 ml) dry
white wine or vermouth

6 cups (48 fl oz/1.5 l)
chicken stock (page 117)
or prepared low-sodium
chicken broth

Kosher salt and freshly
ground white pepper

1 cup (8 fl oz/250 ml)
half-and-half (half cream)

3 pints (3 lb/1.5 kg)
shucked oysters with their
liquor

1 tablespoon minced fresh
rosemary, plus extra for
garnish

In a large soup pot, melt the butter with the oil over medium heat.
Add the onion and celery and sauté until the onion is translucent,
about 3 minutes. Add the wine and cook, stirring occasionally, for
3–4 minutes. Add the stock and season with kosher salt and white
pepper to taste. Reduce the heat to low, cover, and simmer for
about 15 minutes.

Stir the half-and-half into the stock mixture and let simmer,
uncovered, for about 5 minutes. Add the oysters and their liquor
and simmer, uncovered, until the oysters have plumped up and
their edges are curled, about 3 minutes. Stir in the 1 tablespoon
rosemary. Taste and adjust the seasoning.

Ladle the soup into warmed deep bowls and garnish with a bit of
minced rosemary. Serve at once.

MAKES 8–10 SERVINGS

OYSTERS

A traditional holiday food,
oysters are at their best
during the winter months
in most climates. If you live
in an area where oysters
are plentiful, you can shuck
your own for this comforting
stew; you will need about
36 oysters in the shell. If not,
or if you are short on time
during the holidays, use the
shucked oysters sold in
glass jars at fish markets
and good butcher shops.

SPINACH SALAD WITH BLOOD ORANGES AND FENNEL

BLOOD ORANGES

Available in many markets winter through spring, blood oranges have ruby-colored flesh with a raspberry-tinged fragrance and flavor. The amount of red on the skin often indicates the depth of color inside. If blood oranges are not available, you can use tangelos. This cross between a tangerine and a grapefruit or pomelo is in season November through March. It is identifiable by its loose skin; some varieties have a small bump on the stem end. Tangelos are intensely flavored and easy to peel, with few or no seeds.

To make the vinaigrette, in a small bowl, whisk together the balsamic and raspberry vinegars, lemon juice, and olive oil. Season with kosher salt and pepper to taste. Set aside.

Using a large chef's knife, cut off the top and bottom of an orange down to the flesh. Stand the orange upright and cut off the peel in vertical strips to the flesh, following the contour of the fruit. (If using tangelos, simply peel by hand.) Cut the flesh crosswise into thin slices and remove the hard, white center and any seeds. Repeat with the remaining oranges. Cut the fennel bulb in half lengthwise and cut out the core. Cut each half lengthwise into thin slices.

Put the spinach leaves in a large bowl. Add the oranges, fennel, and red onion. Whisk the vinaigrette, add most of it to the salad, and toss well to coat. Taste and adjust the amount of the vinaigrette and the seasoning. Transfer the salad to a large serving bowl or platter or divide among individual plates. Sprinkle with the reserved minced fennel fronds and serve at once.

MAKES 8–10 SERVINGS

FOR THE VINAIGRETTE:

2 teaspoons balsamic vinegar

1 teaspoon raspberry vinegar

1 teaspoon fresh lemon juice

⅓ cup (3 fl oz/80 ml) extra-virgin olive oil

Kosher salt and freshly ground pepper

4 blood oranges or tangelos, about 1½ lb (750 g)

1 fennel bulb, trimmed, fronds minced and reserved for garnish

10 oz (315 g) spinach leaves, preferably baby spinach leaves, well washed (page 50)

½ small red onion, cut crosswise into very thin slices

RED OAKLEAF AND FRISÉE SALAD
WITH PERSIMMONS

FOR THE VINAIGRETTE:

⅓ cup (3 fl oz/80 ml) extra-virgin olive oil

2 tablespoons fresh mint leaves

1½ tablespoons white wine vinegar or pear vinegar

1 teaspoon honey

Kosher salt and freshly ground white pepper

Leaves from 3–4 heads red oakleaf lettuce

Leaves from 1 head frisée lettuce

2 Fuyu persimmons, peeled, seeded if necessary, and cut into thin wedges

Seeds from ½ pomegranate (page 70)

½ cup (2½ oz/75 g) hazelnuts (filberts), toasted and skinned *(far right)*

To make the vinaigrette, in a blender, combine the olive oil and mint and purée until smooth. Add the vinegar and honey and blend until incorporated. Pour the vinaigrette into a small bowl and season with kosher salt and white pepper to taste.

Tear the oakleaf and frisée leaves into bite-sized pieces and put them in a large bowl. Add the persimmons. Whisk the vinaigrette, add most of it to the salad, and toss well to coat. Taste and adjust the amount of the vinaigrette and the seasoning. If serving the salad family style, add the pomegranate seeds and hazelnuts and toss. Or, divide the salad among individual salad plates and sprinkle each serving with pomegranate seeds and hazelnuts. Serve at once.

Variation Tip: If you cannot find fresh pomegranates, substitute ⅓ cup (1½ oz/45 g) dried cranberries.

MAKES 8–10 SERVINGS

TOASTING AND SKINNING HAZELNUTS

In a small, dry frying pan, toast the hazelnuts (filberts) over medium-low heat, stirring frequently, until they begin to turn a deeper brown and are fragrant, 3–5 minutes. Pour the nuts onto a kitchen towel and fold the towel over them. Let sit for 2–3 minutes, then rub the hazelnuts together vigorously inside the towel to loosen the skins. Pour into a colander and shake, letting the skins fall into the sink.

WATERCRESS AND ENDIVE SALAD
WITH WARM BACON VINAIGRETTE

BELGIAN ENDIVE

A member of the chicory family with a faint bitter taste, Belgian endive (chicory/witloof) is at its best during the coldest months. This cylindrical-shaped vegetable is grown in darkness to keep its crisp, curved leaves pale in color. If you have trouble finding the rarer red-tipped variety, you may use the more common pale yellow–tipped endive. The leaves can be stuffed with fillings as an hors d'oeuvre or cut into shreds to add crispness to winter salads. The heads can also be braised or grilled and served as a side dish.

Core each of the endive heads, then halve crosswise and slice very thinly. In a large bowl, combine the watercress, endive, onion, and radishes. Set aside.

To make the vinaigrette, in a frying pan, heat 1 tablespoon of the olive oil over medium heat. Add the bacon and cook until crisp, about 5 minutes. Using a slotted spoon, transfer the bacon to paper towels to drain. Reserve the frying pan and the bacon fat.

Just before serving the salad, place the reserved pan over medium heat and add the remaining 2 tablespoons olive oil. Heat until you can smell the bacon fat and oil, 1–2 minutes. Remove the pan from heat (this is important, as the vinegar can flame up over a gas burner). Add the vinegar and sugar and stir to combine. Pour the vinaigrette over the salad and toss immediately to coat well and partially wilt the leaves. Season with kosher salt and pepper to taste and toss again. Taste and adjust the seasoning.

Divide among warmed salad plates and sprinkle with the bacon pieces and the pecans, if using. Serve at once.

Note: To toast the pecans, in a small, dry frying pan, stir the pecans frequently over medium-low heat until fragrant, 3–5 minutes. Immediately transfer to a bowl and let cool.

MAKES 8-10 SERVINGS

3 heads Belgian endive (chicory/witloof), preferably red

3 bunches watercress, stemmed

¼ sweet red or white onion, thinly sliced

1 bunch multicolored or red radishes, thinly sliced

FOR THE VINAIGRETTE:

3 tablespoons extra-virgin olive oil

2 slices bacon, finely chopped

1½ tablespoons distilled white or red wine vinegar

1 teaspoon sugar, or to taste

Kosher salt and freshly ground pepper

½ cup (2 oz/60 g) pecan halves, toasted (optional, see Note)

THE MAIN COURSE

During the holidays, main courses celebrate abundance and the joy of feasting with family and friends. The following recipes include traditional fare—turkey and dressing, roast goose, baked ham, a brisket braised in red wine, standing rib roast—plus a couple of surprises—roast pork stuffed with dried fruits and rack of lamb accompanied with a cranberry-chile relish.

ROAST BRINED TURKEY WITH
CORN BREAD AND SAUSAGE DRESSING

BRINING

Brining is the answer to the perennial question of how to roast a turkey long enough to cook the dark meat through while not overcooking the white meat. The brine will tenderize and flavor the meat, so the bird no longer has to be partly roasted upside down (hard to do with large birds), in a paper sack, in an aluminum foil tent, or by any of the other methods that supposedly keep the white meat moist. If you do not have a pot large enough to hold the turkey during brining, use a large ice chest and add a small bag of ice to the brine.

Rinse the turkey inside and out under cold running water. Pull out and discard the excess fat and any feather ends. Choose a stockpot large enough to hold the turkey and fit inside your refrigerator. Fill the pot one-third full with cold water. Stir in the kosher salt, sugar, onion, thyme, and peppercorns. Add the turkey, breast side down, and fill with more water so it reaches as far above the turkey as possible. Cover with the lid and refrigerate for 24 hours.

Two hours before roasting, remove the turkey and discard the brine. Rinse the turkey inside and out under cold running water. Return the turkey to the pot and add cold water to cover. Let stand at room temperature to remove some of the brine from the bird.

To roast the turkey, position a rack in the lower third of the oven and preheat to 425°F (220°C). Drain the turkey and pat dry with paper towels inside and out. Slide your fingers between the skin and breast to loosen the skin. Spread half of the softened butter under the skin over the breast, then insert about 12 large sage leaves under the skin, spacing them evenly. Season the neck and body cavities with pepper (do not salt, as the bird was brined). Place the remaining sage sprigs in the body cavity.

Truss the turkey, if desired (page 113). Turn the bird on its back and rub all over with the remaining softened butter. Place the bird, breast side up, on a rack in a large flameproof roasting pan. In a bowl, combine the melted butter and oil to use for basting.

Pour 1 inch (2.5 cm) of water into the bottom of the pan. Reduce the oven temperature to 325°F (165°C) and roast the turkey for 3–3 ½ hours, basting the turkey every hour with the butter mixture and adding water to the pan if needed. Begin testing for doneness after 2½ hours. An instant-read thermometer inserted into the thickest part of the thigh (but not touching bone) should register

1 fresh turkey, preferably organic, about 14 lb (7 kg), neck, heart, and gizzard reserved for turkey stock (page 117)

3 cups (1½ lb/750 g) kosher salt

½ cup (4 oz/125 g) sugar

1 small yellow onion, chopped

1 bunch fresh thyme

1 tablespoon peppercorns, cracked

4 tablespoons (2 oz/60 g) unsalted butter, at room temperature, plus 4 table-spoons unsalted butter, melted

1 bunch fresh sage

Freshly ground pepper

½ cup (4 fl oz/125 ml) olive oil

FOR THE CORN BREAD AND SAUSAGE DRESSING:

Day-old corn bread (far right), crumbled

2 tablespoons unsalted butter

2 tablespoons olive oil

3 sweet Italian sausages, removed from casings

1 small yellow onion, finely chopped

3 celery stalks with leaves, finely chopped

3 large eggs, beaten

1 teaspoon dried thyme, crumbled

Fine sea salt and freshly ground pepper

2 tablespoons minced fresh flat-leaf (Italian) parsley

About 1½ cups (12 fl oz/ 375 ml) turkey stock (page 117)

FOR THE GRAVY:

⅓ cup (2 oz/60 g) all-purpose (plain) flour

½ cup (4 fl oz/125 ml) dry white vermouth

1½ cups (12 fl oz/375 ml) turkey stock, plus chicken stock (page 117) or prepared low-sodium broth if needed

Fine sea salt and freshly ground pepper

165°F (74°C), and the juices should run clear when the thigh is pierced with a knife. Transfer the turkey to a carving board, cover loosely with aluminum foil, and let rest for 30 minutes. While the turkey is roasting, make the stock (page 117) and dressing.

To make the dressing, butter a 9-by-13-inch (23-by-33-cm) baking dish. Put the corn bread in a large bowl. In a large frying pan, melt the butter with the oil over medium heat. Add the sausages and cook, stirring occasionally, until lightly browned, about 5 minutes. Add the onion and cook until translucent, 2–3 minutes. Add the sausage mixture and celery to the corn bread and toss well. Stir in the eggs, thyme, ½ teaspoon sea salt, ½ teaspoon pepper, and the parsley. Stir in as much of the stock as needed to make a moist mixture. Transfer to the prepared dish and cover with aluminum foil. About 45 minutes before the turkey is done, place the dressing in the oven and bake for 45 minutes. Remove the foil and bake until lightly browned and crisp on top, about 20 minutes longer.

To make the gravy, pour the drippings from the turkey roasting pan into a large glass measuring pitcher. Let the fat rise to the surface, then pour or spoon off all the fat, reserving ¼ cup (2 fl oz/ 60 ml). Return the reserved fat to the pan. Place the pan over 2 burners and turn the heat to medium. Stir in the flour and cook, stirring constantly, for 2–3 minutes. Add the vermouth and stir to scrape up the browned bits from the pan bottom. Add enough stock to the drippings to make 2 cups (16 fl oz/500 ml) and add to the pan. Cook, stirring frequently, until the gravy thickens, about 5 minutes. Add more stock, if needed, and sea salt and pepper to taste.

Carve the turkey (page 114) and serve with the gravy and dressing.

MAKES 8–10 SERVINGS, WITH LEFTOVER TURKEY

(Photograph appears on following page.)

CORN BREAD

Preheat the oven to 400°F (200°C). Butter an 8-inch (20-cm) square glass baking dish. In a large bowl, mix ¾ cup (4 oz/ 125 g) stone-ground cornmeal, 1 cup (5 oz/155 g) unbleached all-purpose (plain) flour, 1 tablespoon sugar, 1 teaspoon fine sea salt, and ½ teaspoon baking soda (bicarbonate of soda). In a separate bowl, whisk together 2 large eggs; 4 tablespoons (2 oz/60 g) unsalted butter, melted and cooled; and 1 cup (8 fl oz/250 ml) buttermilk. Stir into the dry ingredients, pour into the dish, and bake until golden, about 25 minutes.

BAKED HAM WITH A BROWN SUGAR, RUM, AND CAYENNE GLAZE

GLAZING

In this recipe, a spicy-sweet, flavorful glaze is brushed on the ham during baking to give it a burnished, golden brown appearance and to complement the assertive taste of the meat. It also enriches the pan drippings, which are then used to make a sauce. Brush the glaze on the ham partway through baking, not at the beginning, to prevent the sugar-based mixture from scorching.

Preheat the oven to 350°F (180°C). Using a large, sharp knife, cut off the skin and all but ¼ inch (6 mm) of the fat from the ham, leaving the surface as smooth as possible. Score the top and sides of the ham diagonally in two opposite directions about 1½ inches (4 cm) apart, creating a diamond pattern. Stick a clove into the corners of each diamond. Place the ham on a rack in a roasting pan. Add the apple juice and 2 cups (16 fl oz/500 ml) water to the pan. Bake the ham for 2 hours. After 1 hour, add more water to the pan if needed.

Meanwhile, make the glaze: In a bowl, combine the brown sugar, rum, kosher salt, and cayenne pepper to taste and stir until smooth. Let stand for about 10 minutes for the sugar to dissolve partially. Remove the ham from the oven and brush the glaze evenly over the ham; reserve the leftover glaze. Return the ham to the oven and bake for about 1 hour longer, brushing it with more glaze every 15 minutes, for a total baking time of about 3 hours. An instant-read thermometer inserted near the center (but not touching bone) should register 130°F (54°C) and the glaze should be golden brown. Transfer the ham to a platter, cover loosely with aluminum foil, and let rest for 15–30 minutes.

Meanwhile, pour the liquid from the roasting pan into a fat separator or a large glass measuring pitcher. Let the fat rise to the surface, then pour or spoon off as much fat as possible. Float a piece of paper towel on the surface to absorb the remaining fat. Pour the degreased liquid into a small saucepan and add any remaining glaze to make a sauce. Set aside.

Carve the ham (page 114). Rewarm the sauce and pour it into a sauceboat. Garnish the platter with the orange wedges and thyme and serve the ham warm with the sauce.

MAKES 8–10 SERVINGS

1 partially cooked bone-in ham, about 12 lb (6 kg)

Whole cloves for studding

2 cups (16 fl oz/500 ml) unfiltered apple juice

FOR THE GLAZE:

1½ cups (10½ oz/330 g) firmly packed light brown sugar

½ cup (4 fl oz/125 ml) dark rum

Pinch of kosher salt

⅛–¼ teaspoon cayenne pepper

Orange or tangerine wedges or fresh or candied kumquats for garnish

Fresh thyme sprigs for garnish

ROAST GOOSE WITH CHESTNUT AND LEEK STUFFING

Remove the neck and giblets from the goose; rinse them and set aside. Remove any excess fat from the body cavity. Rinse the goose inside and out under cold running water. Pat dry with paper towels inside and out. Season the neck and body cavity with kosher salt. Set aside at room temperature while making the stock.

In a saucepan, make the goose stock by combining the neck, heart, and gizzard with the celery, carrot, and onion. Add water to cover, about 3 cups (24 fl oz/750 ml), and a pinch of kosher salt. Bring to a simmer over low heat and cook, uncovered, until well flavored, about 30 minutes. Strain, reserving the stock and discarding the giblets. Cook the liver in a small saucepan of salted simmering water for 10 minutes; Drain and let cool. Chop finely.

Meanwhile, make the stuffing. If using fresh chestnuts, cut an X in the flat side of each one with a small, sharp knife. Put the chestnuts in a saucepan of cold water, bring to a boil over high heat, and cook for 1 minute. Remove from the heat. Using a slotted spoon, remove 2 or 3 chestnuts at a time and peel off their shells and inner skins. Return any that can't be peeled to the hot water; after the others have been peeled, boil them again for 1 minute and peel. Transfer the peeled chestnuts to a saucepan and add water to cover by 1 inch (2.5 cm). Add a pinch of kosher salt and the bay leaf. Bring to a low simmer, cover, and cook until cooked through but firm, about 45 minutes. Drain, reserving the cooking liquid. Let the chestnuts cool to the touch, then chop coarsely and set aside. If using bottled chestnuts, chop coarsely and set aside.

Preheat the oven to 425°F (220°C). In a frying pan, melt the 3 tablespoons butter over medium heat. Add the leeks and sauté until translucent, 2–3 minutes. Transfer the leeks to a large bowl, add the chestnuts, bread crumbs, chopped goose liver, parsley, melted butter, 1 teaspoon sea salt, ½ teaspoon white pepper, and

CHESTNUTS

Sweet and rich, chestnuts are a perfect accompaniment to many holiday dishes. Unlike other nuts, they contain a high amount of starch and little oil, and so are often treated as a vegetable and almost always cooked. Preparing fresh chestnuts—which must be cooked, peeled, and then cooked again—takes time and determination, but their superior flavor can be worth the effort. However, high-quality bottled chestnuts, especially those from France, are a good substitute and can be a great time-saver.

1 goose, about 10 lb (5 kg)

Kosher salt

1 celery stalk with leaves, coarsely chopped

1 carrot, peeled and coarsely chopped

½ small yellow onion, coarsely chopped

FOR THE STUFFING:

1½ lb (750 g) fresh chestnuts or 4 cups (1½ lb/750 g) drained bottled chestnuts

Kosher salt

1 bay leaf, if using fresh chestnuts

3 tablespoons unsalted butter, plus 4 tablespoons (2 oz/60 g) unsalted butter, melted

2 large leeks, white and pale green parts only, chopped and rinsed (page 49)

2 cups (4 oz/125 g) coarse fresh bread crumbs (page 92)

¼ cup (⅓ oz/10 g) minced fresh flat-leaf (Italian) parsley

Fine sea salt and freshly ground white pepper

½ teaspoon dried thyme, crumbled

About 1 cup (8 fl oz/250 ml) chicken stock (page 117) or prepared low-sodium chicken broth, if using bottled chestnuts

⅓ cup (3 fl oz/80 ml) dry white vermouth

⅓ cup (3 fl oz/80 ml) brandy, dry Marsala, or Madeira

the thyme. Stir in as much of the reserved chestnut-cooking liquid or chicken stock as needed to make a moist mixture.

Pack the stuffing loosely into the body cavity of the goose. Truss the goose (page 113). Using a fork, prick the skin on the thighs, back, and lower breast, but do not pierce the flesh. Place the goose, breast side up, on a rack in a flameproof roasting pan. Roast the goose for 15 minutes, then reduce the oven temperature to 350°F (180°C). Roast for 2½–3 hours longer, basting the goose every 30 minutes with ¼ cup (2 fl oz/60 ml) boiling water (to help melt the fat beneath the skin) and siphoning off the fat in the pan bottom with a bulb baster. An instant-read thermometer inserted into the thickest part of the breast (but not touching bone) should register 165°F (74°C), and the juices should run clear when a thigh is pierced with a knife. Do not overcook. Transfer the goose to a carving board, remove and discard the string, and cover loosely with aluminum foil while making the sauce.

Pour the drippings from the roasting pan into a large fat separator or large glass measuring pitcher. Let the fat rise to the surface, then pour or spoon off as much fat as possible. Float a piece of paper towel on the surface to absorb the remaining fat. Return the degreased liquid to the pan. Place the pan over 2 burners and turn the heat to medium. Add the vermouth and stir to scrape up the browned bits from the pan bottom. Add about 2 cups (16 fl oz/ 500 ml) of the reserved goose stock and cook, stirring frequently, until reduced to a flavorful sauce. Stir in the brandy and cook for 2–3 minutes. Taste and adjust the seasoning.

Carve the goose (page 114) and serve with the sauce and stuffing.

MAKES 8–10 SERVINGS

(Photograph appears on following page.)

STUFFING VS. DRESSING

The difference between a stuffing and a dressing is that a stuffing is cooked inside the bird, while a dressing is baked in a dish alongside it. Both have pros and cons. Stuffing is usually moister, as it absorbs juices from the roasting bird. However, an unstuffed bird will cook more quickly, so the meat is less likely to dry out. If you do stuff the bird, be sure the stuffing reaches 165°F (74°C) on an instant-read thermometer, and remove all of the stuffing at serving time.

STANDING RIB ROAST WITH YORKSHIRE PUDDING

One 4-rib standing beef roast, about 8 lb (4 kg), at room temperature

Canola or grapeseed oil for coating

Freshly ground black pepper

2 teaspoons dried thyme, crumbled

FOR THE SAUCE:

¾ cup (6 fl oz/180 ml) heavy (double) cream

½ cup (¾ oz/20 g) minced fresh flat-leaf (Italian) parsley

½ cup (4 oz/125 g) crème fraîche (page 121)

3–4 tablespoons prepared horseradish

Kosher salt and freshly ground white pepper

FOR THE YORKSHIRE PUDDING:

1 cup (5 oz/155 g) unbleached all-purpose (plain) flour

¾ teaspoon fine sea salt

1 cup (8 fl oz/250 ml) milk, at room temperature

3 large eggs, at room temperature

Rub the roast all over with the oil. Sprinkle with black pepper and thyme, rubbing them into the meat. Place the roast, fat side up, on a wire cake rack set in a large cast-iron frying pan.

Place a rack in the lower third of the oven and preheat to 500°F (260°C). Roast the beef for 15 minutes, then reduce the temperature to 325°F (165°C). Roast until an instant-read thermometer inserted into the center of the meat (but not touching bone) registers 140°F (60°C) for medium-rare, about 2 hours longer. Transfer the roast to a carving board, cover loosely with aluminum foil, and let rest while making the Yorkshire pudding.

While the beef is roasting, make the sauce: In a blender, combine the cream and parsley and purée until smooth. Transfer to a deep bowl, add the crème fraîche, and beat with a balloon whisk until soft peaks form. Whisk in the horseradish. Season with kosher salt and white pepper to taste. Cover and refrigerate. Stir before serving.

To make the Yorkshire pudding, raise the oven temperature to 425°F (220°C). Spoon off all but about 3 tablespoons of the fat from the frying pan. Preheat the pan in the oven and prepare the batter: In a bowl, combine the flour and sea salt and stir to blend. Make a well in the center, add the milk, and whisk until blended. Add the eggs and whisk until well blended and bubbly. Pour the batter into the hot frying pan and bake for 10 minutes. If the pudding is not rising evenly, rotate the pan. Bake until puffed and golden brown, about 10 minutes longer.

If not carving the roast at the table, slice the beef a few minutes before the pudding is done and arrange it on a warmed platter. Whisk the sauce a few times and spoon into a sauceboat to serve alongside the meat. Serve the Yorkshire pudding immediately, in its pan, as it will deflate quickly.

MAKES 8–10 SERVINGS

YORKSHIRE PUDDING

Made from the same batter used for popovers, Yorkshire pudding is baked in a large pan with some of the drippings from the roasted meat. (It is also the savory version of the puffed pancake known as a Dutch baby.) Traditionally, Yorkshire pudding was baked under a piece of meat that was roasted on a spit, so the drippings flavored the top of the pudding. Along with horseradish sauce, it is a classic accompaniment to roast beef.

ROAST PORK LOIN STUFFED WITH DRIED FRUITS

In a bowl, combine the dried apricots, prunes, and dried apples. Add the boiling water and stir. Let stand for about 30 minutes, stirring several times. Drain and set aside.

Preheat the oven to 325°F (165°C). Cut a pocket down the length of the roast, cutting halfway through the meat. Insert the dried fruits into the pocket. Using kitchen string, tie the roast closed every 1½ inches (4 cm) or so. Pat the roast dry with paper towels and coat it with oil. Season all over with kosher salt and pepper.

Place the roast, fat side up, on a rack in a flameproof roasting pan. Roast for 1 hour, then test for doneness. An instant-read thermometer inserted into the thickest part of the meat (but not touching the fruit) should register 160°F (71°C). The meat should still be faintly pink in the center. Transfer the roast to a carving board, remove and discard the string, cover loosely with aluminum foil, and let rest while making the sauce.

Tilt the pan and spoon off and discard as much excess fat as possible. Place the pan over 2 burners and turn the heat to medium. Add the stock and Port and stir to scrape up the browned bits from the pan bottom. Cook, stirring frequently, until reduced to a flavorful sauce, about 10 minutes.

To carve the roast, cut it against the grain into slices about ¼ inch (6 mm) thick. Transfer the slices to a warmed platter and serve with the sauce. Or, carve the roast at the table and place it on a warmed platter; pour a little of the sauce over the meat and serve the rest alongside.

MAKES 8–10 SERVINGS

½ cup (3 oz/90 g) dried apricots

½ cup (3 oz/90 g) pitted prunes

½ cup (1½ oz/45 g) dried apples or ½ cup (3 oz/90 g) dried pears

1 cup (8 fl oz/250 ml) boiling water

1 boneless pork loin roast, 4–5 lb (2–2.5 kg)

Canola or grapeseed oil for coating

Kosher salt and freshly ground pepper

½ cup (4 fl oz/125 ml) chicken stock (page 117) or prepared low-sodium chicken broth

¼ cup (2 fl oz/60 ml) Port or apple juice

PORT

Taking its name from the city of Porto, in northern Portugal, the place from which it was first shipped, Port is available in both ruby and tawny types. Tawny Port is golden and is aged much longer than deep-red ruby Port. The finest of these sweet fortified wines, meant for drinking in small glasses after dinner, are produced in Portugal from a single vintage and aged for months to years. For cooking, use an inexpensive domestic ruby Port, which imparts fruity flavor and rich color to sauces and desserts.

RACK OF LAMB WITH CRANBERRY-CHILE RELISH

½ cup (4 fl oz/125 ml) fresh tangerine juice

¼ cup (2 fl oz/60 ml) canola or grapeseed oil

Kosher salt and freshly ground pepper

3 racks of lamb, about 2½ lb (1.25 kg) each, trimmed and frenched (see Note)

FOR THE RELISH:

2 unpeeled tangerines, scrubbed

1 cup (4 oz/125 g) fresh or frozen cranberries

½ large white onion, coarsely chopped

⅓ cup (3 fl oz/80 ml) rice vinegar

¼ cup (¼ oz/7 g) packed fresh mint leaves

1 small jalapeño chile, coarsely chopped

3 tablespoons sugar, or to taste

Pinch of kosher salt

In a large, shallow dish, combine the tangerine juice and oil and season with kosher salt and pepper. Add the lamb and turn to coat the racks on all sides. Let stand at room temperature for about 1 hour, turning occasionally.

Meanwhile, make the relish: Juice 1 of the tangerines and chop the other coarsely, skin and all; remove any seeds. In a blender or food processor, combine the tangerine juice, chopped tangerine, cranberries, onion, vinegar, mint, and jalapeño and purée until smooth. Pour the mixture into a bowl and add the sugar and kosher salt. Let stand at room temperature for at least 30 minutes or for up to 2 hours.

Preheat the oven to 450°F (230°C). If desired, wrap the ends of the bones with aluminum foil to keep them from burning. Place the lamb racks, bone side down, in a roasting pan. Roast until an instant-read thermometer inserted into the center of the lamb (but not touching bone) registers 125°F (52°C) for rare or 135°F (57°C) for medium-rare, 15–20 minutes. Transfer the racks to a carving board, cover loosely with aluminum foil, and let rest for 10–15 minutes.

Cut the racks between the bones into individual chops. Serve 2 or 3 chops per person, with the relish alongside.

Note: Ask your butcher to "french" the racks by cutting the meat and fat from the rib ends. This makes a neater presentation if you are carving at the table and makes it easier to cut the racks into chops.

MAKES 8–10 SERVINGS

RELISHES
Sweet or savory mixtures that are usually highly flavored, relishes may be prepared from cooked or raw ingredients. These condiments are often served with roasted meats. The relish in this recipe is a variation of the raw cranberry sauce made in a blender or food processor. Brilliant in color and spiced with mint, jalapeño, and tangerines, the relish is also excellent paired with other meats such as roast turkey, pork, and venison.

BRISKET BRAISED IN RED WINE

BRAISING

Ideal for tough cuts of meat, such as beef brisket, braising means to simmer food slowly in a moderate amount of liquid. First, the meat is seared in oil on the stove top to brown it evenly on all sides, providing color and contributing flavor. Then liquid and flavorings, such as onions and herbs, are added to the pan, which is covered to prevent the liquid from evaporating and cooked on the stove top over low heat or in a low oven. The moist heat and long, slow cooking ensure that the meat will emerge meltingly tender, accompanied with flavorful pan juices that can be reduced to make a rich sauce.

Preheat the oven to 325°F (165°C). Pat the brisket dry with paper towels. In a large, heavy Dutch oven or flameproof casserole, heat the olive oil over medium-high heat. Add the brisket and brown well on both sides, about 8 minutes total. Using a large fork, transfer the meat to a platter.

Reduce the heat to medium. Add the butter and stir until melted, then add the onion, carrot, celery, and garlic and cook, stirring occasionally, until the onion is tender and golden, 8–10 minutes.

Remove the pan from the heat, add the wine and brandy, place over high heat, and bring to a boil. Stir to scrape up the browned bits from the pan bottom. Turn off the heat and stir in the tomato paste, 1 teaspoon kosher salt, ¼ teaspoon pepper, the thyme, and the bay leaf. Return the brisket to the pan and add the broth. Bring to a simmer over medium heat. Cover the pan tightly and transfer to the oven. Cook until the brisket is fork-tender, 3–3½ hours, turning the meat over after 1 hour and again after 2 hours.

Transfer the brisket to a carving board and cut the meat against the grain into diagonal slices. Overlap the slices on a warmed deep platter and cover with aluminum foil.

Skim the fat from the pan juices. Strain the vegetables and pan juices through a fine-mesh sieve set over a saucepan, pressing on the vegetables with the back of a large spoon to force some of the pulp into the pan. Set the pan over medium-high heat, bring to a simmer, and cook, stirring occasionally, until reduced to a thick, flavorful sauce, 15–20 minutes. Taste and adjust the seasoning. Pour the sauce over the sliced brisket and serve hot.

Note: When sold in butcher shops, whole briskets are usually cut into two pieces, with the first (or flat) cut the leaner of the two.

MAKES 8–10 SERVINGS

1 first-cut (flat-cut) brisket, 4–5 lb (2–2.5 kg) (see Note)

3 tablespoons olive oil

2 tablespoons unsalted butter

1½ cups (7½ oz/235 g) finely chopped yellow onion

½ cup (2½ oz/75 g) finely chopped carrot

½ cup (2½ oz/75 g) finely chopped celery

3 cloves garlic, minced

1½ cups (12 fl oz/375 ml) dry red wine

¼ cup (2 fl oz/60 ml) brandy

1 tablespoon tomato paste

Kosher salt and freshly ground pepper

½ teaspoon dried thyme, crumbled

1 bay leaf, crumbled

2 cups (16 fl oz/500 ml) prepared low-sodium beef broth

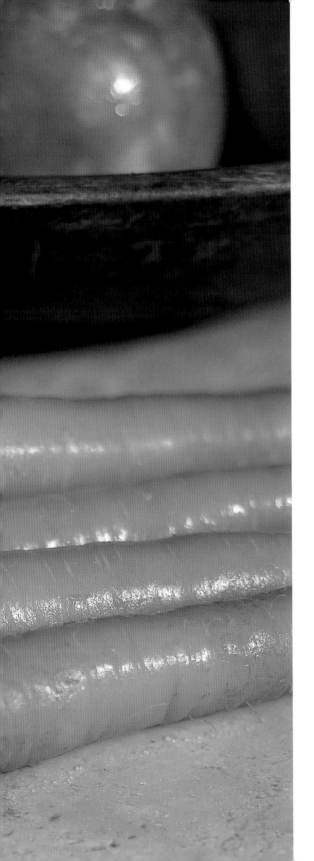

SIDE DISHES

To round out your bountiful feast, serve a selection of side dishes. Here you'll find recipes that make the most of winter vegetables and grains—from acorn squash and leeks to celery root (celeriac) and wild rice—and that complement a range of main courses.

BAKED ACORN SQUASH WITH
MAPLE SYRUP AND BALSAMIC VINEGAR

Preheat the oven to 375°F (190°C). Place the squash halves, cut side up, in a large baking dish. In a small bowl, stir together the maple syrup, vinegar, and lemon juice. Using a pastry brush, brush some of the mixture over the cut surfaces of the squashes.

Bake for about 20 minutes, then brush the squashes again with the maple syrup mixture. Divide any remaining mixture among the squash cavities and add 1 teaspoon butter to each. Sprinkle nutmeg lightly over the squashes.

Return to the oven and bake until the squashes are tender when pierced with a knife, about 20 minutes longer. Serve warm.

MAKES 8 SERVINGS

4 acorn squashes, about 6 lb (3 kg) total weight, halved lengthwise and seeded

½ cup (4 fl oz/125 ml) maple syrup

¼ cup (2 fl oz/60 ml) balsamic vinegar

2 tablespoons fresh lemon juice

8 teaspoons unsalted butter

Freshly grated nutmeg

BALSAMIC VINEGAR

Balsamic vinegar is prized by cooks for its unique combination of sweet, mellow, and acidic flavors. The finest ones come from the Emilia-Romagna region of Italy, where they are produced from white Trebbiano grapes and aged in barrels made from different aromatic woods. The thick, complexly flavored elixir is used in small amounts as a condiment. Less-expensive younger vinegars can be used in salad dressings or combined with other ingredients to make a glaze, as in this recipe for baked acorn squash.

GRATINÉED LEEKS

6 large leeks, about 4 lb
(2 kg) total weight,
trimmed to 8 inches
(20 cm) long and halved
lengthwise, then crosswise

1 cup (8 fl oz/250 ml)
chicken stock (page 117)
or prepared low-sodium
chicken broth

¼ cup (2 fl oz/60 ml) dry
white vermouth

Kosher salt and freshly
ground white pepper

½ cup (2 oz/60 g) shredded
Gruyère cheese

¼ cup (1 oz/30 g) grated
Parmesan cheese

2 tablespoons unsalted
butter, cut into small
pieces

Preheat the oven to 350°F (180°C). Butter a 2-qt (2-l) flameproof gratin dish.

Hold each leek under cold running water and rinse between the leaves to remove all the dirt *(right);* drain well.

Lay the leeks, cut side up, in the prepared dish. Pour the stock and vermouth over them. Season with kosher salt and white pepper. Cover the dish with aluminum foil and bake until the leeks are tender, about 30 minutes. Remove from the oven.

Preheat the broiler (grill). Uncover the dish and sprinkle the Gruyère and then the Parmesan evenly over the leeks. Dot with the butter. Place the dish under the broiler 3–4 inches (7.5–10 cm) from the heat source and broil (grill) until the top is golden brown, about 2 minutes. Serve warm.

MAKES 8–10 SERVINGS

LEEKS

Because leeks are grown in sandy soil, grit collects in the pale green leaves just where they begin to separate from the white part. Since many recipes use both the white and pale green portions, it's important to rinse leeks carefully. Some recipes specify to halve the leek lengthwise and rinse between each leaf under cold running water. If chopped leeks are called for, chop them first and immerse the pieces in a bowl of cold water, letting the grit settle to the bottom. Lift the leeks off with a slotted spoon and repeat as needed with fresh water.

CREAMED SPINACH

In a large stockpot, melt the butter with the oil over medium-low heat. Add the spinach; if using prewashed spinach, sprinkle it with a little water. Cover and cook, stirring once or twice, until the spinach is wilted and bright green, about 5 minutes.

Season with kosher salt and white pepper to taste and sprinkle with the flour. Cook, stirring frequently, to cook off some of the raw flour taste, 2–3 minutes. Stir in the crème fraîche and cook, stirring frequently, until slightly thickened, about 5 minutes. Taste and adjust the seasoning.

Transfer to a warmed serving dish and serve at once.

Variation Tip: For creamed spinach that can be prepared in advance, cook in a covered pot as directed, but without the butter and oil. Rinse under cold water in a colander. Squeeze by hand to remove as much moisture as possible, then mince finely and set aside for up to 5 hours. Cook the spinach in the butter and oil until heated, sprinkle with salt and pepper, and add the flour and then the crème fraîche, as directed. Cover and keep warm in a low 200°F (95°C) oven for up to 30 minutes before serving.

MAKES 8-10 SERVINGS

WASHING SPINACH

Prewashed and trimmed spinach in plastic bags is a great convenience, but if you prefer to buy it by the bunch, be sure to wash it thoroughly: Trim the stems off each bunch. Fill a sink or pot with cold water and plunge the spinach, 1 bunch at a time, into the water. Swish the spinach around in the water, then transfer the spinach to a large bowl or pot. Pour off the water and rinse out any sand, then repeat 2 or 3 times until no sand is left in the bottom of the sink or pot. If the stems are tough, fold the leaves in half lengthwise and strip or cut the stem away along the folded edge.

2 tablespoons unsalted butter

2 tablespoons canola or grapeseed oil

5 bunches spinach, about 5 lb (2.5 kg) total weight, stemmed, well washed *(far left)*, and still wet, or 2½ lb (1.25 kg) prewashed spinach leaves

Kosher salt and freshly ground white pepper

2 tablespoons all-purpose (plain) flour

1 cup (8 oz/250 g) crème fraîche (page 121) or 1 cup (8 fl oz/250 ml) heavy (double) cream

MASHED POTATOES AND CELERY ROOT

2 large celery roots
(celeriacs), about 2 lb (1 kg)
total weight, peeled and
cut into slices 1 inch
(2.5 cm) thick

2½ lb (1.25 g) russet
potatoes, peeled and cut
into slices 1 inch (2.5 cm)
thick

Kosher salt

¾ cup (6 fl oz/180 ml)
half-and-half (half cream)

3 tablespoons unsalted
butter

Freshly ground white
pepper

Put the celery roots and potatoes in separate large saucepans. Add water to cover and a large pinch of kosher salt to each pan. Bring both to a boil over high heat, reduce the heat to low, cover, and simmer until the vegetables are tender, about 20 minutes. Just before they are done, place an ovenproof serving bowl in a 200°F (95°C) oven. (There is no need to preheat the oven.)

In a small saucepan, combine the half-and-half and 2 tablespoons of the butter over low heat and heat until the butter melts. Turn off the heat and cover to keep warm.

Drain the potatoes and celery root. Return the potatoes and celery root to one of the large saucepans and set over medium-low heat; shake the pan until the vegetables begin to stick to the bottom. Remove from the heat.

Pass the vegetables through a ricer into the warmed serving bowl. Alternatively, pass the vegetables through a food mill, or mash them in the pan with a potato masher. Stir in the warm half-and-half mixture. Season with kosher salt and white pepper to taste. Using a rubber spatula, scrape down the sides of the bowl and swirl the top of the purée. Top with the remaining 1 tablespoon butter and serve at once. If necessary, keep warm in a 200°F (95°C) oven for 15–20 minutes, or cover the bowl and set it in a pan of hot water.

MAKES 8–10 SERVINGS

CELERY ROOT

Also known as celeriac, celery root is a knobby, round winter vegetable that contributes a subtle celery flavor to purées when cooked and a crisp crunch to salads when used raw. In this recipe, celery root is mashed with potatoes, giving the dish a lighter texture than if potatoes alone were used, and an interesting, fresh taste that matches well with full-flavored foods such as roast turkey. Both peeled celery root and potatoes discolor quickly when exposed to air and should be immersed in water if not cooked at once to prevent discoloring.

ROASTED ROOT VEGETABLES WITH SHALLOTS AND THYME

Preheat the oven to 400°F (200°C). Prepare all the vegetables for roasting. If using small potatoes, halve them. If using medium potatoes, peel and cut them into wedges ½ inch (12 mm) thick. If using small turnips, peel but leave them whole. If using large turnips, peel and cut them into wedges ½ inch (12 mm) thick. Peel the parsnips and carrots, then halve them lengthwise and cut into pieces 2 inches (5 cm) long. Trim and core the fennel bulbs, then cut lengthwise into wedges ½ inch (12 mm) thick.

In a large gratin dish or roasting pan, combine the potatoes, turnips, parsnips, carrots, fennel, and shallots. Add the olive oil and use your hands to toss the vegetables, coating them evenly. Season with kosher salt and pepper and toss again to coat evenly.

Roast the vegetables, stirring every 10 minutes with a wooden spoon so they brown evenly, until almost tender, 30–40 minutes. Sprinkle with the garlic and thyme and stir well. Roast until all the vegetables are golden brown and tender when pierced with a knife, about 15 minutes longer. Serve warm.

Variation Tip: Instead of thyme, use minced fresh or crumbled dried rosemary or sage, or a mixture of any of these herbs.

MAKES 8-10 SERVINGS

SHALLOTS

A relative of the onion, shallots indeed resemble miniature onions with a russet brown skin. Their flavor is milder, however, and they are a classic ingredient in many traditional French dishes. Because they are small and keep well in a cool, dark place, shallots are often more convenient to use when only a small amount of onion is needed. When roasted in the oven, either on their own or combined with other root vegetables, shallots are transformed into mellow, caramelized nuggets.

16 small unpeeled red potatoes, each about 2 inches (5 cm) in diameter, or 8 medium unpeeled red potatoes, about 4 lb (2 kg) total weight

8–10 unpeeled baby turnips, about ¾ lb (375 g) total weight, or 2 large turnips, about 1 lb (500 g) total weight

2 large parsnips

4 carrots, about 1½ lb (750 g) total weight

2 fennel bulbs

16 large shallots, about 3 lb (1.5 kg) total weight

3 tablespoons olive oil

Kosher salt and freshly ground pepper

3 large cloves garlic, minced

1 tablespoon minced fresh thyme, or 1 teaspoon dried thyme, crumbled

LATKES WITH PEAR-CHERRY CHUTNEY

FOR THE CHUTNEY:

1 lb (500 g) Anjou pears, peeled, cored, and cut into ⅓-inch (9-mm) chunks

½ cup (3½ oz/105 g) firmly packed light brown sugar

½ cup (2½ oz/75 g) dried tart cherries

1 teaspoon peeled and minced fresh ginger

3 tablespoons pear vinegar or red wine vinegar

Pinch *each* of cayenne pepper, ground allspice, and kosher salt

1 tablespoon fresh lemon juice

FOR THE LATKES:

4 lb (2 kg) russet potatoes

2 large eggs, beaten

4 shallots, minced

½ cup (¾ oz/20 g) minced fresh chives

4 cloves garlic, minced

2 tablespoons all-purpose (plain) flour

Kosher salt and freshly ground white pepper

Canola oil for frying

Crème fraîche (page 121) for serving (optional)

To make the chutney, in a nonaluminum saucepan, combine the pears, brown sugar, dried cherries, ginger, vinegar, cayenne, allspice, kosher salt, and lemon juice. Bring to a boil over medium heat, reduce the heat to medium-low, and cook, stirring frequently, until thickened and no longer liquid, about 15 minutes. Remove from heat, cover, and set aside.

To make the latkes, peel the potatoes and put them in a large bowl of cold water. Using the largest rasps on a box grater-shredder, or using a food processor fitted with the shredding disk, shred the potatoes. Place a large handful of potatoes in the corner of a clean kitchen towel and gather the towel tightly around the potatoes. Holding the towel over a bowl, twist to squeeze out as much of the liquid as possible; place the potatoes in another bowl. Repeat with the remaining potatoes, one handful at a time. Spoon any foam off the top of the potato liquid, then pour off and discard the clear liquid on top, reserving the thick white potato starch in the bottom. Add the potato starch, eggs, shallots, chives, garlic, flour, 1 tablespoon kosher salt, and ⅛ teaspoon white pepper to the shredded potatoes. Stir to blend well.

Line a baking sheet with paper towels. In a large frying pan, heat 1 tablespoon oil over medium-high heat until almost smoking. Spoon ¼ cup (2 fl oz/60 ml) batter into the pan and flatten it with a metal spatula. Repeat to make 3 or 4 latkes. Fry, turning once, until crisp and golden brown, about 3 minutes on each side. Using a slotted metal spatula, transfer the latkes to the prepared pan. Transfer the pan to the oven and turn the oven on to 200°F (95°C). Repeat to cook the remaining latkes, adding more oil as needed and removing the pan from the heat if it becomes too hot.

Serve 2 or 3 latkes per person, topped with a spoonful of chutney and a dollop of crème fraîche, if using.

MAKES 8–10 SERVINGS

LATKES

Foods fried in oil, like these latkes, or potato pancakes, are traditionally served during the Jewish holiday Hanukkah because they recall the story this celebration commemorates: Following a siege of the temple in Jerusalem in 165 B.C., a small oil lamp, filled with only a day's supply of oil, miraculously burned for eight days while the victorious Jews prepared new oil to rededicate the temple. Often, latkes are served with warm, spicy applesauce and sour cream. The winter-fruit chutney and crème fraîche in this recipe are variations on these accompaniments.

WILD RICE PILAF WITH
DRIED CRANBERRIES AND PECANS

Preheat the oven to 375°F (190°C). In a saucepan over medium-low heat, bring the stock to a simmer.

In a heavy 2-qt (2-l) flameproof casserole, melt the butter with the oil over medium heat. Add the shallots and sauté until translucent, 2–3 minutes. Add the rice and stir until the grains are well coated, about 3 minutes. Stir in the simmering stock, dried cranberries, bay leaf, thyme, ½ teaspoon sea salt, and ⅛ teaspoon white pepper. Bring to a simmer, stir, and cover. Transfer the casserole to the oven and bake until all the liquid has been absorbed and the rice is tender, 40–45 minutes.

Remove from the oven. Remove and discard the bay leaf and the thyme sprigs, if used. Taste and adjust the seasoning. Stir in the pecans and parsley. Serve hot or warm.

MAKES 8–10 SERVINGS

RICE TYPES

With its nutty flavor and slightly chewy texture, wild rice is a welcome addition to the winter table. It is not a true rice, but rather the seed of an aquatic grass that still grows wild in the northern Great Lakes area of the United States. In this recipe, wild rice can be mixed with short-grain brown rice, which is chewier and sweeter than long-grain brown varieties.

This pilaf is also delicious when made with all short-grain brown rice; unlike white rice, it has not been processed, so its nutritious outer coating remains intact.

4 cups (32 fl oz/1 l) chicken stock (page 117), vegetable stock, or prepared low-sodium broth

2 tablespoons unsalted butter

1 tablespoon canola or grapeseed oil

3 large shallots, minced

2 cups (12 oz/375 g) wild rice or 2 cups (14 oz/440 g) short-grain brown rice, or a mixture

½ cup (2 oz/60 g) dried cranberries

1 bay leaf

2 fresh thyme sprigs or ¼ teaspoon dried thyme, crumbled

Fine sea salt and freshly ground white pepper

½ cup (2 oz/60 g) pecans, toasted (page 22) and coarsely chopped

¼ cup (⅓ oz/10 g) minced fresh flat-leaf (Italian) parsley

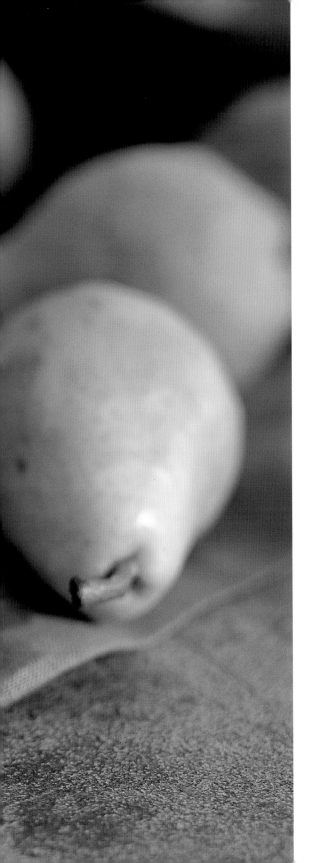

DESSERTS

A holiday dinner is an occasion for an elegant dessert, whether you serve a steamed persimmon pudding or another dish starring winter fruit, such as poached pears. A spicy ginger cake, lavish trifle, intense chocolate cake, or plate of sugar-dusted pastries also makes a sweet ending to the meal.

CHOCOLATE MOUSSE CAKE
62

ENGLISH TRIFLE WITH
PEARS AND DRIED CHERRIES
65

GINGER CAKE WITH ORANGE ZABAGLIONE
66

PERSIMMON-CRANBERRY PUDDING
69

POACHED PEARS WITH CRÈME ANGLAISE
70

ALMOND AND APRICOT RUGELACH
73

CHOCOLATE MOUSSE CAKE

CRÈME CHANTILLY

This French dessert sauce is simply cream beaten until lightly thickened, then sweetened and flavored. Unlike cream that is beaten until peaks form, it is used to gently spoon over foods or to pool onto dessert plates. Combining half heavy (double) cream and half crème fraîche gives the sauce the lightness of whipped cream and the tangy flavor of crème fraîche.

Preheat the oven to 350°F (180°C). Line the bottom of a 9-inch (23-cm) springform pan with parchment (baking) paper. In a metal bowl or the top pan of a double boiler, combine the chocolate and butter. Set snugly over (but not touching) a pan of barely simmering water and melt, stirring occasionally, until smooth. Do not let steam come in contact with the chocolate. Remove from the heat and set aside to cool for about 10 minutes.

In a large bowl, whisk the whole eggs and egg yolks together until blended. Add ½ cup (4 oz/125 g) of the granulated sugar and whisk until blended. Stir in the chocolate mixture, then the Kahlúa, vanilla, and kosher salt. In a large bowl, using a balloon whisk, beat the egg whites with the cream of tartar, if using, until soft peaks form. Gradually beat in the remaining ¼ cup (2 oz/60 g) granulated sugar and beat until stiff, glossy peaks form. Stir a large spoonful of the egg whites into the chocolate mixture to lighten it. Using a rubber spatula, gently fold in the remaining whites until just blended. Pour the batter into the prepared pan and smooth the top. Bake until the cake is puffed and set and the top is cracked, about 35 minutes. Transfer the pan to a wire rack and let the cake cool completely, about 3 hours. The center will sink as it cools.

Just before serving, make the crème Chantilly: In a deep bowl, combine the cream and crème fraîche. Whisk just until thick enough for the whisk to leave a path when pulled across the surface. Stir in the confectioners' sugar and vanilla.

To serve, unclasp and remove the pan sides, then run a long, thin icing spatula between the cake and the paper. Carefully slide the cake onto a serving plate. Cut the cake into slices and spoon a large dollop of the cream over each slice. Dust the cream and cake with cocoa powder and serve.

MAKES ONE 9-INCH (23-CM) CAKE. OR 10-12 SERVINGS

6 oz (185 g) bittersweet chocolate, coarsely chopped

½ cup (4 oz/125 g) unsalted butter

2 whole large eggs, plus 4 large eggs, separated, at room temperature

¾ cup (6 oz/185 g) granulated sugar

2 tablespoons Kahlúa

1 teaspoon vanilla extract (essence)

Pinch of kosher salt

¼ teaspoon cream of tartar (if not using a copper bowl; see page 79)

FOR THE CRÈME CHANTILLY:

½ cup (4 fl oz/125 ml) heavy (double) cream

½ cup (4 oz/125 g) crème fraîche (page 121)

2 tablespoons confectioners' (icing) sugar

½ teaspoon vanilla extract (essence)

Unsweetened cocoa powder for dusting

ENGLISH TRIFLE WITH PEARS AND DRIED CHERRIES

1 cup (5 oz/155 g) dried tart cherries

3 Bartlett (Williams') pears

Juice of 1 lemon

2 cups (20 oz/625 g) raspberry jam

¼ cup (2 fl oz/60 ml) warm water

1 cup (4½ oz/140 g) slivered almonds, toasted (see Note)

Sponge Cake (page 117) or one 9-by-5-inch (23-by-13-cm) bakery pound cake

1 cup (8 fl oz/250 ml) sherry (preferably amontillado or oloroso), Madeira, or sweet Marsala

2 recipes (4 cups/32 fl oz/1 l) Crème Anglaise (page 70)

FOR THE WHIPPED CREAM:

1½ cups (12 fl oz/375 ml) heavy (double) cream

1½ tablespoons confectioners' (icing) sugar

1 teaspoon vanilla extract (essence)

Put the dried cherries in a small bowl and add boiling water to cover. Let stand for at least 30 minutes to plump the cherries. Drain. Reserve about 2 tablespoons of the cherries for garnish.

Peel the pears, halve lengthwise, core, and cut the pears crosswise into thin slices. Put them in a bowl, add the lemon juice, and toss to coat. In a small bowl, combine the jam with the warm water and stir. Reserve about 2 tablespoons almonds for garnish.

Cut the sponge cake into slices ½ inch (12 mm) thick. In a 2½-qt (2.5-l) trifle dish or deep glass bowl, make a layer of one-third of the cake slices, cutting and fitting them together as necessary. Sprinkle the cake layer with one-third of the sherry. Dollop one-third of the jam mixture over the cake. Sprinkle the jam with one-third *each* of the pears, cherries, and almonds, in that order. Pour 1⅓ cups (11 fl oz/330 ml) of the crème anglaise over the top. Repeat to make 2 more layers.

Cover the bowl with plastic wrap and refrigerate the trifle for at least 2 hours or for up to overnight.

About 30 minutes before serving, make the whipped cream: In a deep bowl, using a balloon whisk, beat the cream, confectioners' sugar, and vanilla until soft peaks form. Spoon the cream over the top of the trifle. Garnish with the reserved cherries and almonds. Let stand at room temperature for about 30 minutes. To serve, scoop out large spoonfuls, going down to the bottom layer.

Note: To toast the slivered almonds, in a small, dry frying pan over medium-low heat, stir the almonds frequently until they are fragrant and begin to turn golden brown, 2–3 minutes. Immediately transfer to a bowl and let cool.

MAKES 10–12 SERVINGS

SHERRY

A fortified wine that originated in Spain, sherry is produced in a variety of styles. Fino and manzanilla are dry, pale, and crisp and are served chilled. Amontillado is a lightly sweet, caramel-colored sherry, while oloroso, or cream sherry, is darker in color and sweeter in taste; it is traditionally served at room temperature. Many of the firms in the sherry and Port trade are British, so both these spirits are classic ingredients in English dishes, including trifle—sponge cake soaked in sherry and topped with fruit and custard sauce.

GINGER CAKE WITH ORANGE ZABAGLIONE

ORANGE ZABAGLIONE

To make the zabaglione, a well-loved Italian dessert sauce, for this recipe, in a saucepan over high heat, bring 1 inch (2.5 cm) of water to a boil, then reduce the heat so only a few bubbles rise from the pan bottom. In a stainless-steel or unlined copper bowl, whisk 1 whole large egg, 3 large egg yolks, and ¼ cup (2 oz/60 g) granulated sugar until frothy. Place the bowl over the simmering water and add the grated zest of 1 orange, ¼ cup (2 fl oz/60 ml) fresh orange juice, and 2 tablespoons *each* dry Marsala and Cointreau. Whisk constantly until thick enough to mound when dropped from the whisk, 6–8 minutes.

Preheat the oven to 350°F (180°C). Butter the bottom and sides of an 8-inch (20-cm) springform pan. Line the bottom with a round of parchment (baking) paper or waxed paper. Butter the paper. Dust the paper and the sides of the pan with flour, tapping out the excess. In a small bowl, combine the buttermilk and fresh ginger. Set aside.

Sift together the flour, baking soda, ground ginger, cinnamon, sea salt, cloves, allspice, and pepper together onto a piece of waxed paper. In a large bowl, using a whisk or an electric mixer on medium speed, beat the butter and brown sugar together until light and fluffy. Stir in the molasses. Beat in the eggs, then the rum and vanilla, until smooth. Gradually stir the dry ingredients into the butter mixture until smooth. Stir in the buttermilk mixture until blended.

Pour the batter into the prepared pan and smooth the top. Bake until a skewer inserted into the center comes out clean, 25–30 minutes. Transfer the pan to a wire rack and let the cake cool for 10 minutes. Remove the sides of the pan. Invert the cake onto the wire rack and remove the pan bottom and the paper. Turn the cake right side up and let it cool slightly or completely.

Just before serving, make the zabaglione.

Cut the cake into slices and top each with a spoonful of the warm zabaglione. Sprinkle with candied ginger. Serve the remaining zabaglione in a sauceboat alongside.

Make-Ahead Tip: The cake may be made up to 1 day ahead and served at room temperature.

MAKES ONE 8-INCH (20-CM) CAKE, OR 8-10 SERVINGS

½ cup (4 fl oz/125 ml) buttermilk, at room temperature

1 tablespoon peeled and grated fresh ginger

1½ cups (7½ oz/235 g) unbleached all-purpose (plain) flour

½ teaspoon baking soda (bicarbonate of soda)

2 teaspoons ground ginger

1 teaspoon ground cinnamon

½ teaspoon fine sea salt

¼ teaspoon *each* ground cloves and ground allspice

Pinch of freshly ground pepper

½ cup (4 oz/125 g) unsalted butter, at room temperature

½ cup (3½ oz/105 g) firmly packed light brown sugar

½ cup (5½ oz/170 g) light molasses

2 large eggs, at room temperature

1 tablespoon dark rum

1 teaspoon vanilla extract (essence)

Orange Zabaglione *(far left)*, made just before serving

Minced candied (crystallized) ginger for garnish

PERSIMMON-CRANBERRY PUDDING

3 large, very ripe Hachiya persimmons

1 tablespoon baking soda (bicarbonate of soda)

1½ cups (7½ oz/235 g) unbleached all-purpose (plain) flour

½ teaspoon fine sea salt

1 teaspoon ground cinnamon

1 teaspoon freshly grated nutmeg

4 tablespoons (2 oz/60 g) unsalted butter, at room temperature

1½ cups (10½ oz/330 g) firmly packed light brown sugar

3 large eggs

¼ cup (2 fl oz/60 ml) dark rum or Cointreau

2 tablespoons fresh lemon juice

Grated zest of 1 orange

Grated zest of 1 lemon

1 teaspoon peeled and minced fresh ginger

1½ cups (6 oz/185 g) fresh or frozen cranberries, chopped

1 cup (4 oz/125 g) black walnuts or pecans, chopped

Place a small heatproof bowl upside down in the bottom of a large steamer or stockpot. Add water to almost cover the bowl. Butter a 3-qt (3-l) metal pudding mold. Cut the persimmons in half and spoon the pulp into a blender or food processor. Purée until very smooth. You should have 1½ cups (12 fl oz/375 ml) purée. Transfer the purée to a bowl. Stir in the baking soda and set aside; the mixture will thicken.

In a bowl, combine the flour, sea salt, cinnamon, and nutmeg and stir to blend. In a large bowl, using a whisk or an electric mixer on medium speed, beat the butter and brown sugar together until light and fluffy. Beat in the eggs, rum, and lemon juice. Stir in the purée. Gradually stir the dry ingredients into the persimmon mixture until smooth. Stir in the orange and lemon zests, ginger, cranberries, and nuts.

Bring the water in the pot to a simmer over medium heat. Pour the batter into the prepared mold and smooth the top; the mold should be about two-thirds full. Cover tightly with the lid or with a piece of aluminum foil secured with kitchen twine. Put the mold on the bowl in the pot, cover the pot, and steam for about 2½ hours, checking the pan every hour to add more water as needed. To test, uncover the pudding; the top should spring back when lightly touched. Transfer the mold to a wire rack and let the pudding rest in the mold for about 15 minutes. Unmold the pudding onto a warmed serving plate, cut into wedges, and serve warm.

Serving Tips: Accompany wedges of the warm pudding with spoonfuls of a lemon version of crème Chantilly. Follow the instructions on page 62, but substitute the grated zest of 1 lemon and 1 tablespoon fresh lemon juice for the vanilla. Garnish with finely shredded orange zest and surround with candied or fresh cranberries and orange slices.

MAKES 12 SERVINGS

PERSIMMONS

The large, heart-shaped Hachiya persimmon *(shown front)* must be very soft to the touch for the flesh to taste sweet. To hasten ripening, place the fruit in a closed paper bag for 2 or 3 days. Hachiyas are puréed and used in desserts like this pudding. Or, freeze them whole and eat with a spoon for a simple sorbet. The short, squat Fuyu persimmon *(shown back)*, eaten when hard and crisp, adds sweetness and color to salads (page 21), appetizer plates, and cheese plates. If you live in an area where wild persimmons grow, you can use 10–12 wild persimmons in place of the Hachiyas in this recipe.

POACHED PEARS WITH CRÈME ANGLAISE

To make the crème anglaise, rinse the inside of a nonaluminum saucepan with water and shake out the excess water. Pour in the milk and place over medium-low heat until small bubbles form around the edges of the pan, about 5 minutes. In a small bowl, combine the whole eggs, egg yolk, and granulated sugar and whisk just until blended. Gradually whisk in half of the hot milk, then pour the egg mixture into the pan. Reduce the heat to low and cook, stirring constantly, until thick enough to coat the back of spoon, leaving a clear trail when a finger is drawn through it, 6–8 minutes. Do not allow to boil. Strain through a fine-mesh sieve into a bowl. Stir in the vanilla. Cover with plastic wrap, pressing it directly on the surface to prevent a skin from forming, and let cool. Refrigerate for at least 2 hours or for up to 2 days.

With an apple corer or a small, sharp knife, carefully core each pear from the bottom. Leaving the stems intact, peel the pears. In a large nonaluminum stockpot, combine the pomegranate juice, brown sugar, lemon zest and juice, and cinnamon stick. Bring to a boil over high heat, then reduce the heat to a simmer. Place the pears on their sides in the liquid and cook, uncovered, for 10–15 minutes. Carefully turn the pears over and cook until a small knife can be inserted easily into the bottom of a pear, 10–15 minutes longer.

Remove the pears and stand upright on individual plates. Remove and discard the cinnamon. Pour about 2 cups (16 fl oz/500 ml) of the pan liquid into a small saucepan. Simmer over medium-low heat until reduced by half, about 10 minutes. Gradually whisk in the Cointreau mixture, reduce the heat to low, and simmer, stirring, until the sauce thickens to a glaze, about 10 minutes. Pour a little glaze over each pear, then spoon some crème anglaise around each one. Sprinkle with the pomegranate seeds and garnish with mint sprigs. Serve the remaining glaze alongside.

MAKES 8–10 SERVINGS

FOR THE CRÈME ANGLAISE:

2 cups (16 fl oz/500 ml) milk

2 large eggs, plus 1 egg yolk

¼ cup (2 oz/60 g) granulated sugar

2 teaspoons vanilla extract (essence)

8–10 firm but ripe Bartlett (Williams') pears, 3–3¾ lb (1.5–1.8 kg) total weight, bottoms trimmed so they stand upright

6 cups (48 fl oz/1.5 l) bottled pomegranate juice

1 cup (7 oz/220 g) firmly packed light brown sugar

Julienned zest and juice of 1 lemon

1 cinnamon stick

2 tablespoons Cointreau or other orange liqueur, mixed with 1 tablespoon cornstarch (cornflour)

Seeds from 1 pomegranate (far left)

12 fresh mint sprigs

ALMOND AND APRICOT RUGELACH

FOR THE DOUGH:

4 oz (125 g) natural cream cheese, at room temperature (see Note)

½ cup (4 oz/125 g) unsalted butter, at room temperature

1 cup (5 oz/155 g) unbleached all-purpose (plain) flour

¼ cup (2 oz/60 g) granulated sugar

Grated zest of ½ lemon

2 teaspoons fresh lemon juice

½ teaspoon almond extract (essence)

Pinch of fine sea salt

½ cup (5 oz/155 g) apricot jam

¾ cup (3½ oz/105 g) slivered almonds, finely chopped

1 large egg, beaten

Confectioners' (icing) sugar for dusting

To make the dough, in a food processor, combine the cream cheese, butter, flour, granulated sugar, lemon zest and juice, almond extract, and salt and pulse until the dough begins to pull away from the bowl. To make by hand, in a bowl, combine the cream cheese and butter. Using a wooden spoon, stir until smooth and blended. Add the flour, granulated sugar, lemon zest, lemon juice, almond extract, and sea salt and stir until a soft dough forms.

Turn the dough out onto a lightly floured board and form into a ball. Divide into 4 pieces and flatten each into a disk. Stack the disks in a zippered plastic bag and refrigerate for at least 1 hour or for up to overnight.

Preheat the oven to 350°F (180°C). Line 2 baking sheets with parchment (baking) paper.

On a lightly floured board, roll out a disk into a round about 8 inches (20 cm) in diameter and ⅛ inch (3 mm) thick. Spread evenly with 2 tablespoons of the jam, then sprinkle evenly with one-fourth of the almonds. Using a large chef's knife, cut the round into 8 wedges. Starting at the wide end, roll each wedge toward the point. Transfer the pastries, point sides up, to the prepared sheets, spacing them about 2 inches (5 cm) apart. Repeat to use the remaining dough and filling.

Using a pastry brush, brush the top of each rugelach with the beaten egg. Bake until golden brown, about 25 minutes. Let the pastries cool on the baking sheets for 5 minutes, then transfer to wire racks. Dust very lightly with confectioners' sugar and let cool completely.

Note: Natural cream cheese, without added stabilizers or gums, is available in natural-food stores.

MAKES 32 PASTRIES

RUGELACH

In some Jewish traditions, dairy foods are eaten during Hanukkah, for they honor the story of Yehudith, who escaped a lascivious Greek ruler by plying him with dairy foods and wine until he fell asleep. To continue the dairy theme for a holiday dessert, serve these rugelach, pastries made with a cream cheese dough, with ice cream, rice pudding, or ricotta cheese pudding.

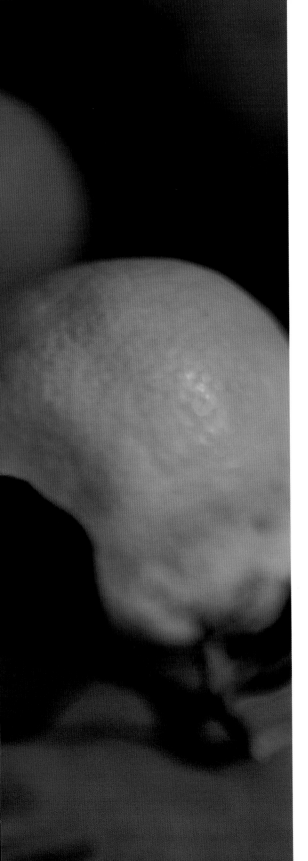

HOLIDAY BREAKFAST

Holiday mornings call for special breakfast treats, whether billowy souffléd omelets, special French toast, or hearty chicken hash. For accompaniments, serve warm almond scones and the best of the cold season's citrus fruits, made into a sweet curd or beautiful compote.

PANETTONE FRENCH TOAST
76

SOUFFLÉD OMELET WITH PARMESAN
79

CHICKEN HASH
80

ALMOND SCONES WITH TANGERINE CURD
83

CITRUS COMPOTE
84

PANETTONE FRENCH TOAST

PANETTONE

This spongy golden Italian egg bread, studded with dried fruits, is a treasure to have on hand for holiday breakfasts and teas. The sweet bread is popular in Italy year-round, but especially during the holidays. Because of the high egg and butter content, panettone will keep for several days after opening.

Excellent panettones are available in specialty-food shops during the holidays, packaged in tall, tapering cardboard boxes, often wrapped in bright foil. Serve panettone sliced, untoasted or toasted, with jams or citrus curd (page 83), or use it to make this special French toast.

Cut the panettone into 12–15 vertical slices, each 1 inch (2.5 cm) thick, then cut all but the end slices in half.

In a bowl, whisk the eggs until just blended, then whisk in the milk, orange zest and juice, Cointreau, almond extract, granulated sugar, cinnamon, and nutmeg to taste. Pour into a large shallow bowl or dish (you may need 2 bowls) and place the bread slices in the mixture. Soak for about 10 minutes on each side.

In each of 2 large sauté pans or frying pans, melt 1 teaspoon of the butter with 1 teaspoon of the oil over medium heat. When the butter foams, add some of the soaked bread slices, taking care not to crowd them. Cook, turning once, until lightly browned, 3–5 minutes on each side. Turn the slices over again and cook them for a few minutes longer on each side until browned to your taste.

Turn off the heat. Using a slotted metal spatula, transfer the French toast to serving plates, place them in the oven, and turn the oven on to 200°F (95°C). Repeat to cook the remaining slices.

Dust the French toast with confectioners' sugar and serve at once, with maple syrup, yogurt, and lemon wedges.

MAKES 8–10 SERVINGS

1 purchased panettone, about 2 lb (1 kg)

6 large eggs

2 cups (16 fl oz/500 ml) milk

Grated zest of 1 orange

1 cup (8 fl oz/250 ml) fresh orange juice

2 tablespoons Cointreau or other orange liqueur

½ teaspoon almond extract (essence)

6 tablespoons (3 oz/90 g) granulated sugar

½ teaspoon ground cinnamon

Freshly grated nutmeg

4–6 teaspoons unsalted butter

4–6 teaspoons canola or grapeseed oil

Confectioners' (icing) sugar for dusting

Warmed maple syrup, plain yogurt, and lemon wedges for serving

SOUFFLÉD OMELET WITH PARMESAN

12 large eggs, separated, at room temperature

½ teaspoon cream of tartar (if not using a copper bowl; *far right*)

Fine sea salt and freshly ground white pepper

¼ cup (1 oz/30 g) plus 2 tablespoons grated Parmesan cheese

2 tablespoons minced fresh flat-leaf (Italian) parsley

4 tablespoons (2 oz/60 g) unsalted butter

Preheat the oven to 400°F (200°C). In a large copper or other metal bowl, using a balloon whisk, beat the egg whites with the cream of tartar, if using, until soft peaks form. Add ½ teaspoon sea salt and beat until stiff, glossy peaks form.

In another large bowl, beat the egg yolks until thick and pale in color. Whisk in ¼ teaspoon white pepper, the ¼ cup (1 oz/30 g) Parmesan, and the parsley. Stir a large spoonful of the egg whites into the yolk mixture to lighten it. Using a rubber spatula, gently fold in the remaining whites just until blended.

In a heavy, 12-inch (30-cm) ovenproof frying pan, melt the butter over medium heat. Spoon in the egg mixture, mounding it in the center. Cook until lightly browned on the bottom, 3–4 minutes (test by lifting an edge with a metal spatula). Sprinkle with the 2 tablespoons Parmesan, transfer to the oven, and bake until set and lightly browned on top, 6–8 minutes. Cut into wedges and serve at once directly from the frying pan.

MAKES 8-10 SERVINGS

BEATING EGG WHITES

Recipes often call for beating egg whites with a small amount of cream of tartar, which stabilizes the beaten whites and maintains their smooth texture. If you use a copper bowl, you can omit the cream of tartar—the metal itself will react with the egg whites to stabilize the foam. Egg whites will mound more quickly and higher when beaten by hand with a balloon whisk rather than by mixer. When beaten to soft peaks, the whites will fall gently over to one side when the whisk is turned upright; when beaten to stiff peaks, they will hold their shape and look glossy.

CHICKEN HASH

If using a half roast chicken, remove and discard the skin and pull the meat from the bones. Cut into ½-inch (12-mm) dice. Set aside. Put the unpeeled whole potatoes in a large pot. Add cold water to cover and a large pinch of kosher salt. Bring to a low boil over high heat, reduce the heat to medium, cover partially, and let simmer briskly until the potatoes are tender when pierced with a knife, about 25 minutes. Drain the potatoes and let cool to the touch, then peel and cut them into ½-inch (12-mm) dice. Set aside.

In a small saucepan, bring the stock to a brisk simmer over medium-high heat and cook until reduced to about 1 cup (8 fl oz/ 250 ml), about 10 minutes. In another small saucepan, melt the butter over medium-low heat. Stir in the flour and cook, stirring constantly, about 3 minutes; do not let brown. Whisk in the reduced stock and cook, whisking constantly, until the mixture thickens to a gravy, about 3 minutes. Season with kosher salt and black pepper to taste. Remove from the heat and set aside.

In a large frying pan, heat the oil over medium heat. Add the bacon and cook until crisp, 1–2 minutes. Using a slotted spoon, transfer the bacon to paper towels to drain. Reserve the fat in the pan.

Heat the bacon fat over medium heat for about 1 minute. Add the potatoes and cook, stirring occasionally and scraping up any browned bits from the pan bottom, until the potatoes are lightly browned, about 10 minutes. Add the chicken, green onions, bell pepper, pimentón, turmeric, cayenne, and black pepper to taste. Cook, stirring frequently, until the green onions are wilted and the chicken is heated through, about 5 minutes. Stir in the bacon and as much chicken gravy as needed to make a moist mixture. Cook for 2–3 minutes longer. Taste and adjust the seasoning. Stir in the parsley. Serve hot.

MAKES 8–10 SERVINGS

PAPRIKA AND PIMENTÓN

Made from ground dried pimiento peppers, paprika imparts color and flavor to savory foods. Although the pimiento is always sweet, it ranges in both color and piquancy. As a result, paprika is widely available in three versions: mild, or sweet; hot; and very hot. Look for Hungarian paprika, considered to be the best, in a bright red tin. Pimentón, a Spanish spice made from smoked pimientos, is also available sweet, hot, or very hot. It gives savory dishes a subtle smoky flavor.

½ large purchased rotisserie-roasted chicken, or about 2 cups (12 oz/375 g) diced leftover cooked chicken or turkey meat

3 lb (1.5 kg) red potatoes

Kosher salt

1½ cups (12 fl oz/375 ml) chicken stock (page 117) or purchased low-sodium chicken broth

1½ tablespoons unsalted butter

1½ tablespoons all-purpose (plain) flour

Freshly ground black pepper

3 tablespoons canola or grapeseed oil

1 slice bacon, finely chopped

8 green (spring) onions, including tender green parts, coarsely chopped

1 red bell pepper (capsicum), seeded and diced

½ teaspoon hot or sweet pimentón or Hungarian paprika

¼ teaspoon ground turmeric

Pinch of cayenne pepper or red pepper flakes

2 tablespoons minced fresh flat-leaf (Italian) parsley

ALMOND SCONES WITH TANGERINE CURD

FOR THE CURD:

**1 large whole egg, plus
4 large egg yolks**

⅓ cup (3 oz/90 g) sugar

Pinch of kosher salt

Grated zest of 1 tangerine

**¾ cup (6 fl oz/180 ml) fresh
tangerine juice**

**6 tablespoons (3 oz/90 g)
cold unsalted butter**

FOR THE SCONES:

**2½ cups (12½ oz/390 g)
unbleached all-purpose
(plain) flour**

**½ cup (2 oz/60 g) blanched
almonds, finely ground, plus
¼ cup (1 oz/30 g) sliced
(flaked) almonds**

2 tablespoons sugar

1 tablespoon baking powder

¾ teaspoon fine sea salt

**6 tablespoons (3 oz/90 g)
cold unsalted butter**

2 large eggs, beaten

**½ cup (4 fl oz/125 ml) heavy
(double) cream**

**¼ teaspoon almond extract
(essence)**

**1 large egg yolk mixed with
1 tablespoon half-and-half
(half cream)**

To make the curd, in a saucepan, bring 1 inch (2.5 cm) of water to a low simmer over medium-low heat. In a stainless-steel bowl, combine the whole egg, egg yolks, sugar, and kosher salt and whisk to combine. Whisk in the tangerine zest and juice. Place the bowl over the pan of simmering water and whisk until the eggs are warm and begin to thicken, about 3 minutes. Whisk in the butter 1 tablespoon at a time and continue whisking constantly until the mixture is thick enough to form a thick, nondissolving ribbon on the surface when dropped from the whisk, at least 10 minutes total. Remove from the heat and strain through a fine-mesh sieve into a bowl. Cover with plastic wrap, pressing it directly on the surface to prevent a skin from forming, and let cool. Refrigerate for at least 2 hours or for up to 1 week.

Preheat the oven to 425°F (220°C). Line a baking sheet with parchment (baking) paper. To make the scones, in a large bowl, combine the flour, ground almonds, sugar, baking powder, and sea salt and whisk until well blended. Cut the butter into small pieces and add to the dry ingredients. Using a pastry cutter or 2 table knives, cut in the butter until the mixture resembles a coarse meal. In another bowl, whisk the eggs, cream, and almond extract together. Stir into the dry ingredients just until evenly moistened.

Turn the dough out on a floured board, form it into a ball, and knead a few times just until smooth. Pat into a disk about 1 inch (2.5 cm) thick and cut into 12 equal wedges. Transfer the wedges to the prepared pan, spacing them 2 inches (5 cm) apart. Brush the tops lightly with the yolk mixture. Sprinkle each wedge with about 1 teaspoon of the sliced almonds.

Bake until the scones are golden brown on the bottoms and lightly golden on the tops, about 15 minutes. Transfer to a wire rack and let cool for a few minutes. Serve warm, with the tangerine curd.

MAKES 12 SCONES AND 1½ CUPS (12 FL OZ/375 ML) CURD

MAKING CITRUS CURDS

An English delicacy, citrus curds are traditionally spread on warm scones and tea breads or used as a pastry filling. Curds are simple to make: egg yolks and sugar are beaten with citrus juice over hot water until thickened, then the mixture is stabilized by adding butter, which allows it to remain thick when chilled. Although curds can be made in a double boiler pan set, they are easier to make in a stainless-steel bowl set over a pan of simmering water. The larger, wider bowl facilitates whisking. Citrus curd will keep for weeks in the refrigerator, making it a good holiday gift.

CITRUS COMPOTE

Using a large chef's knife, cut off the top and bottom of an orange down to the flesh. Stand the orange upright and cut off the peel in vertical strips to the flesh, following the contour of the fruit. (If using tangelos, simply peel by hand.) Cut the flesh crosswise into slices ¼ inch (6 mm) thick. Remove the hard white center and any seeds. Put the slices in a large nonaluminum bowl. Repeat with the remaining oranges.

Pour the cassis and lemon juice over the oranges and stir to blend. Cover and refrigerate for 30–60 minutes.

To serve, transfer the oranges to a serving dish and sprinkle with the minced mint, orange zest, and the pomegranate seeds, if using. Garnish with mint sprigs and serve.

MAKES 8-10 SERVINGS

12 large blood oranges, navel oranges, or tangelos, or a mixture, about 4 lb (2 kg) total weight

¼ cup (2 fl oz/60 ml) crème de cassis or cassis syrup

2 tablespoons fresh lemon juice

3 tablespoons minced fresh mint, plus mint sprigs for garnish

Zest of 1 orange, removed with a zester (page 104)

Pomegranate seeds (page 70) for garnish (optional)

CRÈME DE CASSIS

Black currants, widely grown in Europe but not common in the United States, give this liqueur its deep black-red color and fruity flavor. Crème de cassis is added to white wine to create the cherry-colored kir cocktail and is excellent combined with fresh fruit. Try it on sliced peaches, plums, and other stone fruits in summer, as well as in this winter citrus compote. Cassis syrup, similar in color and taste but nonalcoholic, is also available though is a bit harder to find. Look for it in specialty-food shops.

OPEN HOUSE

The holidays are the time of year to invite friends and family into your home. To make the gathering even more special, offer an array of savories and sweets, including cheese torta *with smoked salmon, spinach frittata, holiday cookies, and chocolate truffles. Don't forget to toast the season with festive holiday drinks—they're a guaranteed crowd pleaser.*

GOUGÈRES
88

MASCARPONE AND GOAT CHEESE TORTA
WITH SMOKED SALMON
91

STUFFED MUSHROOMS
92

SPINACH FRITTATA
95

HOT SPICED CIDER AND MULLED WINE
96

EGGNOG
99

HOLIDAY SUGAR COOKIES
100

CHOCOLATE TRUFFLES
103

CHRISTMAS CAKE WITH MARZIPAN
104

GOUGÈRES

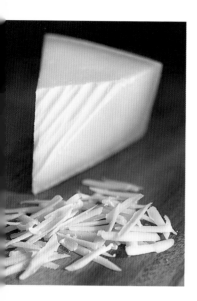

GRUYÈRE

Produced in both France and Switzerland, Gruyère is a cow's milk cheese with a subtle, nutty flavor. It shreds easily and melts beautifully, making it excellent for cooking, and is a superlative table cheese. Swiss Gruyère is one of the traditional cheeses used in fondue. The French version of this cheese, also called Gruyère de Comté, or simply Comté, is aged longer than Swiss Gruyère. Hence, it has a deeper flavor that is preferred for *gougères* and other French dishes.

Place racks in the top and bottom thirds of the oven and preheat the oven to 425°F (220°C). Line 2 baking sheets with parchment (baking) paper. In a heavy saucepan, combine the water, butter, sea salt, cayenne, and paprika. Bring to a boil over medium heat and cook until the butter melts. Remove from the heat and quickly add the flour all at once, beating vigorously with a wooden spoon, until completely blended. Place the pan over medium-high heat and beat until the mixture forms a mass in the center of the pan and the pan bottom begins to be coated with the cooked mixture, 1–2 minutes; do not heat the mixture above lukewarm.

Remove from the heat and use the spoon to make a well in the center of the mixture. Immediately add 1 of the eggs and beat with the spoon until completely blended, then beat in 3 more of the eggs, one at a time. Beat in the Gruyère and one-third of the Parmesan cheese until melted and thoroughly blended.

To form the *gougères*, spoon the paste into a pastry (piping) bag fitted with a plain tip ½ inch (12 mm) in diameter. (If you don't have a pastry bag and tip, use a teaspoon.) Pipe mounds of the paste about 1 inch (2.5 cm) in diameter and ½ inch (12 mm) high onto the prepared sheets, spacing them 2 inches (5 cm) apart.

In a small bowl, beat the remaining egg with the milk. Brush the *gougères* with the egg mixture, taking care not to mash them down, and sprinkle the remaining Parmesan cheese over the tops. Place the sheets on the racks in the oven and bake until the *gougères* are lightly browned and doubled in size, about 20 minutes. Remove from the oven, but leave the oven on. Using a small, sharp knife, cut a small slit in the side of each *gougère*. Return the sheets to the oven for 5 minutes to dry out the inside of the puffs partly. Transfer the *gougères* to wire racks. Serve warm or at room temperature, piled into a large bowl or passed on trays.

MAKES ABOUT 3 DOZEN HORS D'OEUVRES

1 cup (8 fl oz/250 ml) water

6 tablespoons (3 oz/90 g) unsalted butter, cut into small pieces

1 teaspoon fine sea salt

⅛ teaspoon cayenne pepper

¼ teaspoon sweet Hungarian paprika

1 cup (5 oz/155 g) unbleached all-purpose (plain) flour

5 large eggs

¾ cup (3 oz/90 g) shredded Gruyère cheese

¾ cup (3 oz/90 g) grated Parmesan cheese

1 teaspoon milk

MASCARPONE AND GOAT CHEESE TORTA WITH SMOKED SALMON

¼ cup (1 oz/30 g) shelled salted pistachios

6 oz (185 g) mascarpone or natural cream cheese (see Note, page 73), at room temperature

6 oz (185 g) fresh plain goat cheese, at room temperature

Freshly ground white pepper

Olive oil, as needed

½ cup (2 oz/60 g) finely chopped smoked salmon, packed

½ baguette, cut into slices ¼ inch (6 mm) thick

In a small, dry frying pan, stir the pistachios over medium-low heat until lightly toasted and fragrant, about 5 minutes. Pour onto a kitchen towel and fold the towel over them. Let the nuts cool for 2–3 minutes, then rub them together vigorously inside the towel to loosen the skins. Pour into a colander and shake over the sink, letting the skins fall through. Chop the nuts into pieces no larger than ¼ inch (6 mm). Set aside.

In a small bowl, combine the mascarpone and goat cheeses. Season with white pepper to taste and stir until blended and smooth. Line a deep 3- or 4-cup (750-ml or 1-l) rounded bowl or mold with plastic wrap, letting the edges hang over the sides. Lightly oil the plastic wrap. Spoon one-third of the cheese mixture into the bowl. Using an oiled tablespoon, pack it down firmly. Spread the smoked salmon evenly over the cheese, packing it down and leveling the top. Spoon in another third of the cheese, packing it down firmly. Sprinkle most of the pistachios evenly over the cheese, reserving some for sprinkling on top. Spoon in the remaining cheese, packing it down firmly and leveling the top. Cover with the overlapping plastic wrap and refrigerate for at least 2 hours or up to 24 hours.

Preheat the oven to 350°F (180°C). Place the baguette slices in a single layer on a rimmed baking sheet. Toast in the oven until dry on top, about 5 minutes. Turn the slices over and toast on the other side until crisp on the edges but still soft in the center, about 5 minutes longer. Transfer to wire racks and let cool.

To serve, uncover the top of the *torta* and unmold it onto a large serving plate. Remove the plastic and sprinkle the reserved pistachios on top. Let the *torta* stand at room temperature for 1 hour. Arrange the baguette slices around the *torta* and serve.

MAKES 12 SERVINGS

SMOKED SALMON

A delicious luxury, most quality varieties of smoked salmon are cold smoked, a longer, more demanding process than hot smoking. Nova, which once denoted smoked salmon from Nova Scotia, now refers to any cold-smoked Atlantic salmon. Lox is salmon that has been both brine cured and smoked; it is a slightly saltier product. Because this *torta* calls for chopped smoked salmon, you may use slices, the most readily available form, or trimmings or scraps, which are often available in fish markets and specialty-food shops.

STUFFED MUSHROOMS

FRESH BREAD CRUMBS
To make fresh bread crumbs, lay slices of dense-textured country-style bread flat on a countertop and leave overnight to dry out. Or use bread that is several days old. Cut off the crusts, tear the slices into large pieces, then process them in a blender or food processor to the desired texture. You can store fresh bread crumbs in a zippered plastic bag in the refrigerator for up to 4 days.

Preheat the oven to 350°F (180°C). Line a rimmed baking sheet with parchment (baking) paper or butter the baking sheet.

Remove the stems from the mushrooms and reserve. Brush the mushroom caps, inside and out, with the ¼ cup olive oil. Place them, rounded side down, on the prepared pan. Season with kosher salt and white pepper to taste. Set aside.

Using a large chef's knife, chop the mushroom stems as finely as possible. Place the chopped stems in the corner of a clean kitchen towel, gather the towel tightly around the mushrooms, and twist to release as much moisture as possible. Set aside.

In a saucepan, melt the 3 tablespoons butter with the 2 tablespoons oil over medium heat. Add the green onions and sauté until the white parts are translucent, 2–3 minutes. Add the mushroom stems, raise the heat to medium-high, and sauté until lightly browned, 6–8 minutes. Add the Marsala and boil until almost dry, about 5 minutes. Remove from the heat and add the bread crumbs, Gruyère, ½ cup (2 oz/60 g) of the Parmesan, the parsley, paprika, and the ⅓ cup cream. Season with salt and white pepper to taste. Add a little more cream if needed to make a thick mixture.

Spoon the stuffing into the mushroom caps. Sprinkle each with a little of the remaining ¼ cup (1 oz/30 g) Parmesan and drizzle with a little of the melted butter.

Bake until lightly browned on top, 20–25 minutes. Serve warm.

Make-Ahead Tip: These mushrooms can be baked 3 or 4 hours in advance and kept at room temperature. Just before serving, reheat in a 350°F (180°C) oven for about 15 minutes.

MAKES 8-10 SERVINGS

24 large fresh cremini or white button mushrooms, each about 2 inches (5 cm) in diameter, brushed clean

¼ cup (2 fl oz/60 ml) plus 2 tablespoons olive oil

Kosher salt and freshly ground white pepper

3 tablespoons unsalted butter, plus 3 tablespoons unsalted butter, melted

4 green (spring) onions, including tender green parts, finely chopped

½ cup (4 fl oz/125 ml) dry Marsala, sherry, or white vermouth

⅓ cup (¾ oz/20 g) coarse fresh bread crumbs *(far left)*

½ cup (2 oz/60 g) shredded Gruyère cheese

¾ cup (3 oz/90 g) grated Parmesan cheese

½ cup (¾ oz/20 g) minced fresh flat-leaf (Italian) parsley

¼ teaspoon sweet Hungarian paprika

⅓ cup (3 fl oz/80 ml) heavy (double) cream, plus more as needed

SPINACH FRITTATA

2 bunches spinach, about 2 lb (1 kg) total weight, stemmed, well washed (page 50), and still wet, or 1 lb (500 g) prewashed spinach leaves

4 tablespoons (2 oz/60 g) unsalted butter

1 tablespoon olive oil

4 green (spring) onions, including 3 inches (7.5 cm) of the green parts, finely chopped

3 large cloves garlic

10 large eggs

15 oz (470 g) whole-milk ricotta cheese, drained overnight *(far right)*

¼ cup (1 oz/30 g) grated Parmesan cheese

¼ cup (1 oz/30 g) grated pecorino romano cheese

Fine sea salt and freshly ground white pepper

¼ cup (⅓ oz/10 g) minced fresh flat-leaf (Italian) parsley

Preheat the oven to 350°F (180°C). If using prewashed spinach, sprinkle it with a little water. Put the spinach in a large stockpot and place it over medium heat. Cover and cook, stirring once or twice, until the spinach is wilted and bright green, about 5 minutes. Transfer the spinach to a large colander and let stand, stirring occasionally, until cool to the touch.

Squeeze one small handful of spinach at a time over the sink to extract as much liquid as possible and transfer to a cutting board. Using a large chef's knife, mince the spinach finely. Set aside.

In a small frying pan, melt 1 tablespoon of the butter with the oil over medium heat. Add the green onions and garlic and sauté until the whites of the onions are translucent, about 3 minutes. Remove from the heat and set aside.

In a large bowl, whisk the eggs just until blended. Stir in the spinach, green onion mixture, ricotta, Parmesan, pecorino romano, 1½ teaspoons sea salt, ½ teaspoon white pepper, and the parsley.

Heat a heavy, 12-inch (30-cm) ovenproof frying pan, preferably enameled cast iron, over medium-low heat. Melt the remaining 3 tablespoons butter in the pan. When the foaming subsides, add the egg mixture and transfer the pan to the oven. Bake until the frittata is golden brown and firm on top, 30–35 minutes.

Transfer the pan to a wire rack and let cool for 10 minutes. To unmold, place a baking sheet on top of the pan. Holding the sheet tightly against the pan, quickly invert them to unmold the frittata. Lift off the pan. Repeat the process with a large serving plate to invert the frittata so that it is right side up. Let cool to room temperature. Cut into wedges and serve.

MAKES 24 APPETIZER SERVINGS

RICOTTA CHEESE

Fresh ricotta cheese should be drained overnight so it will be as thick as possible; otherwise, the frittata could be watery. To drain ricotta, rinse a double layer of cheesecloth (muslin), wring dry, and use it to line a sieve placed over a deep bowl. Make sure the bottom of the sieve is several inches above the bottom of the bowl. Place the ricotta in the sieve and refrigerate overnight. Then drain off the liquid and use the ricotta as directed in the recipe.

HOT SPICED CIDER

Using a vegetable peeler, cut the zest from three-quarters of the orange and set aside. Cut the orange into quarters so that one quarter contains all the intact zest. Insert the cloves into the skin of the quarter that still has its zest and put it in a large non-aluminum saucepan. Squeeze the juice from the remaining orange quarters into the pan. Add the apple juice, reserved orange zest, lemon zest and juice, and cinnamon stick and bring to a gentle simmer over low heat. Simmer for about 20 minutes. Strain the hot cider and ladle into cups or heatproof glasses. Garnish with cinnamon sticks, if desired, and serve warm.

MAKES 8–10 SERVINGS

1 orange

8 whole cloves

8 cups (64 fl oz/2 l) unfiltered apple juice

Stripped zest of 1 lemon

2 tablespoons fresh lemon juice

1 cinnamon stick, plus extra cinnamon sticks for optional garnish

CLOVES

The dried flower buds of a tropical evergreen tree, cloves impart their deep, almost hot flavor to a variety of holiday dishes, both sweet and savory. Used whole, they're a favorite for studding hams (page 30) while the ground spice is used to flavor seasonal cakes and cookies. The name of these little nail-shaped spices comes from the Latin word *clavus,* for "nail." As directed in these beverage recipes, whole cloves can be stuck into a wedge of citrus or tied in a square of cheesecloth (muslin) with other spices for steeping. Strain the liquid or remove the bundle before serving.

MULLED WINE

Tie the cloves and nutmeg pieces in a small square of cheesecloth (muslin), or put them in a large metal tea ball. In a large non-aluminum pot, combine the wine, sugar, orange and lemon zests, orange and lemon juices, and cinnamon sticks. Add the clove-and-nutmeg bundle. Heat over medium-low heat until steam begins to rise from the pot and the mixture is hot, about 10 minutes; do not let boil. Remove and discard the bundle. Keep the wine warm over very low heat until ready to serve. Ladle into cups or heatproof glasses, garnish with the citrus zest (if using), and serve warm.

MAKES 8–10 SERVINGS

12 whole cloves

2 nutmegs, cracked into pieces with a hammer

2 bottles (750 ml each) dry red wine

½ cup (4 oz/125 g) sugar

Stripped zest from 2 oranges *and* 2 lemons, plus extra zest for garnish (page 104)

¾ cup (6 fl oz/180 ml) fresh orange juice

¼ cup (2 fl oz/60 ml) fresh lemon juice

2 cinnamon sticks

EGGNOG

2 large eggs, separated, at room temperature

⅓ cup (3 oz/90 g) sugar

⅓ cup (3 fl oz/80 ml) dark rum or Cognac

2 tablespoons Grand Marnier or Cointreau

2 cups (16 fl oz/500 ml) whole milk

½ teaspoon vanilla extract (essence)

Grated zest of 1 lemon

¾ cup (6 fl oz/180 ml) fresh orange juice

1 cup (8 fl oz/250 ml) heavy (double) cream

Freshly grated nutmeg

In a saucepan, combine the egg yolks and sugar and whisk until blended. Place the pan over low heat and whisk constantly until the mixture is thick, about 5 minutes. Whisk in the rum and Grand Marnier and cook for 1 minute, then whisk in the milk.

Remove the pan from the heat and stir in the vanilla, lemon zest, and orange juice. In a large bowl, using a balloon whisk, beat the egg whites until soft peaks form. In a deep bowl, using a balloon whisk, beat the cream until soft peaks form when the whisk is turned upright. Whisk 1 large spoonful of the whites into the yolk mixture until well blended. Gently fold in the remaining whites, then gently fold in the whipped cream.

Pour the eggnog into a large glass bowl and sprinkle with nutmeg to taste. (A little nutmeg goes a long way.) Serve at once or cover and refrigerate for up to 3 hours. If making ahead, whisk the eggnog gently to blend before serving. Ladle into small glasses or demitasse cups.

Note: This recipe contains uncooked egg. For more information, see page 121.

MAKES 8–10 SERVINGS

NUTMEG

The oval, brown seed of a tropical evergreen, nutmeg has a warm, sweet flavor. Keep whole nutmeg on hand to use in baked goods, and to grate over drinks, desserts, and some savory foods, such as béchamel sauce. As with other hard spices, the flavor of nutmeg will be more intense when it is freshly grated. Special small graters designed to hold a nutmeg in the top compartment are available, but you can also use the finest rasps of a box grater-shredder.

HOLIDAY SUGAR COOKIES

DECORATING COOKIES

Spoon the colored icings into separate pastry bags. To fill a pastry bag, fit it with a pastry tip. Place the bag, tip down, in a glass, fold the edge over the sides to form a cuff, and fill half full with icing. Unfold the cuff and twist until the bag is taut and the tip is full. Holding the tip at a 45-degree angle, squeeze the bag to pipe the icing. To coat a cookie, pipe an outline, then fill in with icing using a small spatula. If desired, while the base coat on the cookies is still moist, sprinkle with colored sugars, nonpareils, or dragées. If decorating with another color of icing, let the base coat dry before continuing.

In a bowl, combine the flour, baking powder, and sea salt and whisk until well blended. In a separate large bowl, using an electric mixer on medium speed, beat the butter and granulated sugar together until light and fluffy. Beat in the egg, milk, and vanilla until smooth. Gradually stir in the dry ingredients until smooth. Turn the dough out onto a lightly floured board and form into a ball. Divide the dough in half and form each piece into a thick disk, smoothing the edges. Place in a zippered plastic bag and refrigerate for at least 2 hours or for up to 2 days.

Preheat the oven to 350°F (180°C). Remove 1 disk of dough from the refrigerator and let stand on a lightly floured board for about 5 minutes. Pound the disk a few times with a rolling pin to soften. Roll out the dough to a thickness of about ⅛ inch (3 mm), turning it over and dusting it and the board lightly with flour as needed to keep the dough from sticking.

Use cookie cutters to cut out cookies. Then, using a metal spatula, transfer to ungreased baking sheets, spacing them about 1 inch (2.5 cm) apart. Form the dough scraps into a ball, reroll, and cut out more cookies until all the dough is used. (You may need to refrigerate the scraps until firm enough to roll out.) Bake the cookies, 1 sheet at a time, until firm but uncolored on the top and lightly browned on the bottom, about 10 minutes. Using a metal spatula, transfer the cookies to wire racks and let cool completely. Repeat with the second disk of dough.

To make the icing, using a fine-mesh sieve, sift the 1½ cups confectioners' sugar into a bowl. Add the milk and stir until smooth. Add more sifted sugar or milk as needed until spreadable. Divide the icing among separate small bowls. Stir a drop or two of coloring into each bowl, adding more if needed to deepen the color. Decorate the cookies (left), then let the icing dry.

MAKES ABOUT 3 DOZEN COOKIES

2¼ cups (11½ oz/360 g) unbleached all-purpose (plain) flour

1 teaspoon baking powder

½ teaspoon fine sea salt

½ cup (4 oz/125 g) unsalted butter, at room temperature

¾ cup (6 oz/185 g) granulated sugar

1 large egg

2 tablespoons milk

1 teaspoon vanilla extract (essence)

FOR THE ICING:

1½ cups (6 oz/185 g) confectioners' (icing) sugar, plus more as needed

3 tablespoons milk, plus more as needed

Assorted food colorings

CHOCOLATE TRUFFLES

7 oz (220 g) bittersweet chocolate *(far right)*, chopped

¼ cup (2 oz/60 g) crème fraîche (page 121) or ¼ cup (2 fl oz/60 ml) heavy (double) cream

2 tablespoons dark rum, Cognac, Chambord liqueur, Grand Marnier, or Kahlúa (see Note)

1 teaspoon vanilla extract (essence)

1 cup (3 oz/90 g) unsweetened cocoa powder

In a metal bowl or the top of a double boiler pan set, combine the chocolate, crème fraîche, and rum. Set over barely simmering water and cook, stirring occasionally, until the chocolate is melted and the mixture is smooth. Remove from the heat and stir in the vanilla. Cover the pan and refrigerate until the mixture has partially set and can be formed into truffles, about 30 minutes.

Place a fine-mesh sieve over a plate and press the cocoa powder through with the back of a wooden spoon. Remove the truffle mixture from the refrigerator and roll 1 teaspoonful between your palms to make an unevenly shaped ball. Transfer to a baking sheet and repeat to use up the remaining truffle mixture.

Roll each truffle lightly in the cocoa powder. Store the truffles in an airtight container in the refrigerator for up to 1 week. Remove them from the refrigerator 15–30 minutes before serving.

Note: Depending on what liqueur you choose, you can vary the flavor of the truffles. For raspberry, use Chambord, or for orange, use Grand Marnier. Kahlúa will add a coffee flavor.

MAKES ABOUT 3 DOZEN TRUFFLES

CHOCOLATE

Bittersweet chocolate contains anywhere from 35 to 70 percent chocolate liquor. When choosing chocolate for a dish that depends on it for most of its flavor, as with these truffles, look for a brand that lists 70 percent liquor. This will guarantee an intense chocolate taste. To melt chocolate, chop it into coarse pieces with a large chef's knife, then melt the pieces in the top of a double boiler placed over barely simmering water to prevent scorching. Do not allow any moisture to come in contact with the chocolate—this could cause it to seize, or stiffen.

CHRISTMAS CAKE WITH MARZIPAN

ZESTING CITRUS

To make strips of citrus zest, choose organic fruit if possible and scrub it well. Shave off the colored part of the peel with a vegetable peeler or paring knife; don't include the ziste, or white pith, as it is bitter. To grate zest, use the next-to-smallest rasps on a box grater-shredder or a long, narrow grater designed especially for zesting citrus. You can also mince zest strips with a large chef's knife. To create long shreds of zest for a garnish, use a zester; if using the zest as an ingredient in a dish, you may want to mince it with a chef's knife.

Plan to make this cake 6–8 weeks before you want to serve it. To make the candied citrus peel, cut the zest from the oranges and lemons into wide strips with a vegetable peeler *(left)*. Place the zest in a large saucepan and add water to cover. Bring to a boil over medium-high heat, then immediately drain the zest. Repeat twice so that the zest has been boiled in 3 changes of water. Cut the zest into strips ⅛ inch (3 mm) wide, reserving the trimmings. In a large, heavy saucepan, bring ¼ cup (2 fl oz/60 ml) water and the granulated sugar to a boil over medium-high heat. Cook until the sugar dissolves, about 3 minutes. Add the zest strips and trimmings and return to a boil. Cook, uncovered, until the syrup is absorbed and the zest is translucent, about 20 minutes.

Spread the zest pieces out on a baking sheet and let cool. Sprinkle them with some of the superfine sugar, stir, and spread them out again. Let the zest dry for 5 minutes, then stir, sprinkle with the remaining superfine sugar, and spread out. When completely dry, place the zest in a zippered plastic bag or an airtight container. Store indefinitely at room temperature.

To make the cake, using a large chef's knife, finely chop the candied citrus peels, dried fruits, and nuts; dip the knife in hot water so it cuts cleanly. In a large bowl, combine all the chopped ingredients. Add the Cointreau and orange and lemon juices. Stir, cover, and let stand overnight at room temperature.

Preheat the oven to 300°F (150°C). Cut down one fold of a large, clean double-strength brown-paper bag. Cut out and discard the bottom. Draw a circle 17 inches (43 cm) in diameter on the paper and cut out. Place a 9-inch (23-cm) tube pan in the center of the circle, and draw around the base of the pan and the inside of the tube. Fold the circle in half three times, pencil lines outside, and cut off the tip. Unfold the paper and cut along the folds about 4 inches (10 cm) toward the inner circle, stopping at the line. Butter the pan, fit the paper into the pan, and butter the paper.

FOR THE CANDIED CITRUS PEEL:

2 oranges *and* 2 lemons, well scrubbed

½ cup (4 oz/125 g) granulated sugar

2 tablespoons superfine (caster) sugar

FOR THE CAKE:

¼ cup (1½ oz/75 g) *each* candied orange and candied lemon peel

½ cup (2½ oz/75 g) *each* dried black Mission figs and dried Calimyrna figs

1 cup (6 oz/185 g) *each* dried pears and dried apricots

1 cup (5 oz/155 g) dried cherries

¾ cup (4½ oz/140 g) golden raisins (sultanas)

¾ cup (3½ oz/105 g) slivered blanched almonds

¾ cup (3 oz/90 g) pistachios

½ cup (4 fl oz/125 ml) Cointreau or light rum

½ cup (4 fl oz/125 ml) fresh orange juice

1 tablespoon fresh lemon juice

6 tablespoons (3 oz/90 g) unsalted butter, at room temperature

1½ cups (10½ oz/330 g) firmly packed light brown sugar

2 large eggs

1 teaspoon almond extract (essence)

½ teaspoon orange extract (essence) or oil

1 cup (5 oz/155 g) unbleached all-purpose (plain) flour

1 teaspoon baking powder

½ teaspoon fine sea salt

½ teaspoon ground allspice

½ teaspoon freshly grated nutmeg

¼ teaspoon ground cinnamon

¼ teaspoon ground mace

½ cup (4 fl oz/125 ml) brandy or light rum, plus more as needed

FOR THE TOPPING:

7 oz (220 g) marzipan

Slivered almonds, pistachios, and candied citrus peel for garnish

In a large bowl, using a whisk or an electric mixer on medium speed, cream the butter and sugar until light and fluffy. Beat in the eggs and almond and orange extracts. In another bowl, combine the flour, baking powder, sea salt, allspice, nutmeg, cinnamon, and mace and stir to blend. Gradually stir the dry ingredients into the butter mixture. Stir in the dried-fruit mixture and its liquid.

Pour the batter into the prepared pan, smoothing the top with a rubber spatula. Bake until the cake is just beginning to pull away from the sides of the pan, about 2 hours and 20–30 minutes. Transfer the pan to a wire rack and let the cake cool completely; this will take 3–4 hours.

Unmold the cake onto a wire rack and lift off the pan. Remove the paper from the cake and brush the top and sides with some of the ½ cup brandy. Soak a large piece of rinsed and wrung cheesecloth (muslin) in the remaining brandy, lightly wring it out, and wrap it around the cake to cover it completely. Wrap the cake with aluminum foil and place it in a zippered plastic bag. Set in a cool, dark place and let age for 6–8 weeks. Halfway through the aging time, unwrap the cake down to the cheesecloth, sprinkle it well with brandy on all sides, and rewrap the cake.

To add the topping, unwrap the cake completely. Form the marzipan into a disk. On a cool surface, roll the marzipan out into a 9-inch (23-cm) round. Trim the edges. Place the round on top of the cake, pressing it gently, and trim a hole for the center. Place the almonds, pistachios, and candied citrus peel on top of the marzipan in a decorative pattern and press them into the marzipan. To serve, cut the cake into very thin slices and allot 2 or 3 slices per serving.

MAKES ONE 9-INCH (23-CM) CAKE, OR ABOUT 18 SERVINGS

(Photograph appears on following page.)

MARZIPAN

A traditional holiday sweet, marzipan is a fine-textured blend of almond paste, sugar, and frequently egg whites. It is used as a filling or icing for sweet breads and cakes and for making candies in a variety of fanciful shapes— including fruits, vegetables, and animals. Marzipan is available in 7-oz (220-g) cylinders in specialty-food shops and many supermarkets. Make sure your marzipan is fresh; it should be soft and pliable in the package.

CHRISTMAS BASICS

More than any other time of year, the winter holidays call us to entertain at home with friends and family. This is the season to strengthen the bonds of love and kinship that connect us, and cooking and sharing special holiday foods is one of the most enjoyable ways to do so. Since this is also the season when most of us are pressed for time, it's important to plan ahead and to be well organized for entertaining. These tips will help you do just that.

PLANNING A MENU

Begin planning your Christmas, Hanukkah, or New Year's meal a few weeks in advance by designing your menu. When choosing recipes, strive to select foods that will both contrast and harmonize with one another. Don't choose dishes that use the same ingredients or are similar in color and texture; instead, try to balance these elements throughout the meal. Some foods seem to go together naturally, such as roast beef and earthy root vegetables. And, of course, everyone has his or her favorite combinations.

Because holiday meals typically include a number of dishes, choose some recipes that can be prepared completely or partially ahead. For example, most soups, like Butternut Squash and Apple Soup (page 14), can be cooked a day in advance and often taste even better when reheated, after the flavors have had a chance to meld. Many desserts, such as Ginger Cake with Orange Zabaglione (page 66) or Chocolate Mousse Cake (page 62) can be made a day ahead, leaving only the accompanying dessert sauce to be put together at the last minute.

When planning the side dishes, select some that can be cooked on the stove top since the main course will be occupying most, if not all, of the oven space. Some dishes can be baked ahead of time and then rewarmed while the meat rests before carving.

If you want to offer hors d'oeuvres before your guests sit down to dinner, select recipes you can make ahead and serve at room temperature, such as Mascarpone and Goat Cheese Torta with Smoked Salmon (page 91), or that can be rewarmed before serving, such as Stuffed Mushrooms (page 92).

If you are hosting a buffet-style meal, such as an open house, plan dishes that taste their best when served warm or at room temperature. Baked Ham with a Brown Sugar, Rum, and Cayenne Glaze (page 30) and Roasted Root Vegetables with Shallots and Thyme (page 54) would both be fine choices. The Open House chapter (pages 86–107) features a selection of hors d'oeuvres, sweets, and beverages that is perfect for a buffet.

Whatever menu you choose, be careful not to take on more than you can do comfortably. If you are too harried to enjoy entertaining, chances are your guests won't enjoy themselves either. If you are hosting an event with family and close friends, consider asking some of them to bring a dish or to help you in the kitchen. This will ease the pressure so you will have more time to spend with your guests and to enjoy the festivities.

ESTIMATING QUANTITIES

Most of the recipes in this book serve 8 to 10 people. Many can be doubled, though the cooking times for larger pieces of meat, such as turkey, ham, and standing rib roast, will be longer. When serving a large group, consider making two first courses, such as soup and salad, rather than one, as well as several side dishes and desserts. When you offer more than one dish per course, people will usually take smaller portions of each.

GETTING ORGANIZED

Once you have a menu, create a shopping list with two columns: foods that can be purchased ahead, and foods that should be purchased just before using. Order meat or poultry from your butcher at least 1 week in advance. In the case of poultry, seek out fresh organic birds. If you must use frozen, allow 1 to 2 days for thawing the bird in the refrigerator. This is also the time to inventory your pantry staples, such as sugar and flour, and to replenish them so you won't run out at the last minute.

It's a good idea to make a list of all the equipment you will need to prepare the recipes and to serve the meat, including large serving bowls, platters, and serving spoons. This is a chance to fill in the gaps in your kitchenware. Items such as a large carving board, a ricer, a fat separator, and a pastry (piping) bag can make preparing and serving a big meal easier and more pleasant.

Make sure you have enough table space and chairs to accommodate your guests. Inexpensive folding plastic-topped tables, both round and rectangular (to be hidden under floor-length tablecloths), are now available, as are simple wooden folding chairs. Keep in mind you can always rent or borrow tables and chairs (as well as glasses, plates, and utensils), too.

Think about how you want to decorate your table, and jot down some ideas. Make a note to purchase any new items you need, such as tablecloths, napkins, candles, and candleholders.

Finally, make a list of perishable decorations to buy at the last minute, such as flowers and greens. Consider placing seasonal fruits on the table among the candles rather than using a high centerpiece, which can obstruct conversation. Pomegranates, apples (especially Lady apples), pears, Fuyu persimmons, tangerines, kumquats, and nuts are all beautiful, whether used alone or mixed with traditional decorations, such as colored glass balls or fir branches. Sprigs of fresh rosemary, sage, and bay laurel are fragrant green garnishes that can be placed directly on the tablecloth or used to garnish roasts or plates.

A few days before the meal, create a preparation timeline, beginning with tasks that can be completed 2 days ahead, such as making soups; then, those that can be done 1 day ahead, such as dicing bread for stuffing or dressing, or preparing desserts. Finally, draw up a plan of action for the big day itself, with the estimated times for each task, including when to put meat or poultry in the oven. Remember to plan your time carefully; even experienced cooks will have trouble trying to prepare more than 2 or 3 dishes at once. Check temperatures and the size of pans needed for each dish to see whether some can be in the oven at the same time. Remember that some large roasts can rest for up 30 minutes after being removed from the oven, while smaller ones can rest for up to 15 minutes. This gives you time to reheat other foods and to prepare a sauce or gravy at the last minute.

THE MAIN COURSE

While no holiday menu would be complete without delicious side dishes and satisfying desserts, the centerpiece of the feast is still the main course, be it baked ham or roast goose. These tips will help you cook and present the perfect centerpiece. All the main courses in this book are either roasted or braised, which is traditional during the holidays, the time for feasting. These cooking methods also allow the cook time to prepare other foods while the meat or poultry is cooking. Here are some general roasting tips, followed by information about specific types of meat and poultry. (For tips on braising, see page 42.)

ROASTING BASICS

For best results, use a heavy roasting pan, which prevents the pan juices from burning. A roasting rack keeps meat or poultry from overcooking on the bottom and also elevates the food for faster cooking and even browning. Dishes with long roasting times, such as turkey, often specify adding a small amount of water or other liquid to the pan; this will also help keep the juices from burning.

Meat and poultry will cook more evenly if they are at room temperature when roasted. Remove large pieces of meat and poultry, such as a rib roast or a turkey, from the refrigerator 1 hour before roasting.

Roasting is a dry-heat process, which means that if meat is over-cooked, it will be dry. For this reason, one of your most important pieces of holiday kitchenware could be an oven thermometer. Use it to check your oven temperature ahead of time, so you don't ruin the main course by overcooking it in an oven that is too hot.

Begin checking meat or poultry for doneness 30–60 minutes before it is supposed to come out of the oven. Insert an instant-read thermometer into the meat (but not touching bone) to check the temperature. Do not leave the thermometer in the meat.

Keep in mind that the meat will continue to cook after it is removed from the oven, and the temperature can rise by 5°F (3°C) as the meat rests.

Doneness temperatures will vary somewhat for different foods. The United States Food Safety and Inspection Service suggests a minimum temperature of 160°F (71°C) for cooked meat and poultry. This is the temperature needed to destroy harmful bacteria. If you are pregnant, older, have a compromised immune system, are cooking for older people or young children, or want to limit your exposure to bacterial risk, you should observe this rule. However, many people choose to cook red meat to a lower temperature for juicier flesh and fuller flavor. The temperatures in this book for red meats are for rare and medium-rare, so are lower than 160°F (71°C). Cook them longer if you prefer a medium doneness.

When the correct internal temperature is reached, transfer the meat to a carving board and cover it loosely with a tent of aluminum foil. This keeps the food warm and allows the juices, which rise to the surface during roasting, to settle back into the meat and ensure moist results. The meat will also firm up while resting and become easier to carve. Large items, such as a turkey or standing rib

roast, can rest at room temperature for up to 30 minutes; smaller pieces can rest for up to 15 minutes.

POULTRY

To prepare poultry for roasting, remove the neck and giblets, which are usually packed in a paper sack and placed in the cavity. The neck, heart, and gizzard can be used to make stock (pages 32 and 117), and the liver can be poached separately, then chopped and added to the stuffing or gravy later. (If the liver is cooked with the other parts, it can make the stock bitter.)

Rinse the bird with cold water inside and out, then pat it dry with paper towels. Remove any excess fat deposits, found inside the body cavity. If you see any stub ends of feathers and pinfeathers, pull them out with your fingers or with tweezers or needle-nosed pliers.

If you are stuffing the bird, do so just before putting it into the oven. First season the neck and body cavities with salt and pepper, then loosely stuff both of them or just the body cavity. Do not pack in the stuffing; it will expand during cooking. Close the neck and body cavities by trussing the bird with kitchen string or with metal skewers if you are presenting the whole bird at the table.

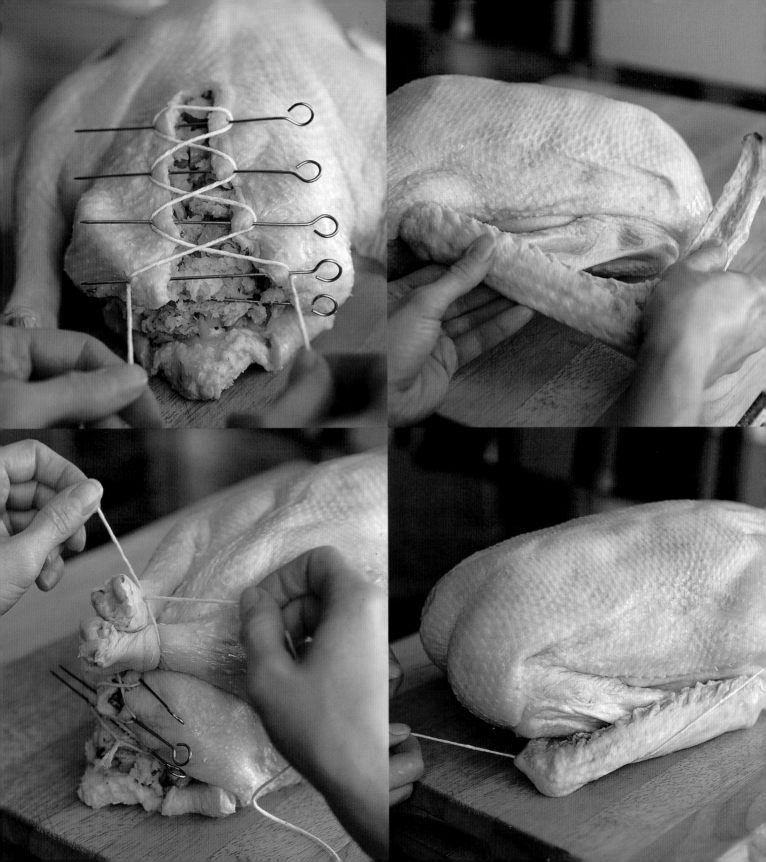

Trussing a bird yields a neat, compact form that makes for an attractive presentation for carving at the table. It also helps hold in the stuffing. Shown opposite and explained below are the basic steps for trussing poultry. Many people prefer to carve the bird in the kitchen and present the slices on platters; in this case, trussing is not necessary, and the bird will actually cook more evenly untrussed.

1 **Closing the cavity:** After the bird (here, a goose) has been stuffed, hold the skin over the body cavity closed and pierce with 4 or 5 metal skewers. Cut a generous amount of kitchen string, and starting at the upper pin, interlace the string back and forth as you would shoelaces. Pull it snug and tie securely at the bottom. Trim the excess string.

2 **Tucking the wings under:** Tuck the first joint of each wing under the body of the bird.

3 **Tying the drumsticks:** Cut a long piece—about 4 feet (4 m)—of kitchen string. Cross the ends of the drumsticks over each other, wind the string around them, and tie the ends together tightly.

4 **Forming a compact shape:** Run the string around the thighs and under the middle of the wings on both sides of the bird, pulling tightly. Keeping the string pulled tight, tie a firm knot around the excess flesh at the neck of the bird and trim off the excess string.

Many recipes call for basting the bird periodically to help brown and crisp the skin and to keep the flesh moist. To baste, while the bird is roasting, pull out the oven rack and brush or spoon the basting liquid over the meat. Basting liquids often are the accumulated pan juices, but they can also be melted butter or a mixture of butter and olive oil. Whatever liquid you use, it should contain some fat, which is a flavor conductor. A bulb baster, also called a turkey baster, will facilitate distributing the liquid over the bird. A metal baster is a better choice than a plastic one, which might be warped or melted by the hot liquid.

To test for doneness, insert an instant-read thermometer into the thickest part of the thigh (but not touching bone). The temperature should reach 165°F (74°C), and the juices should run clear when the thigh is pierced with a knife.

BEEF

Do not salt a beef roast before cooking (salt draws juices to the surface), but freshly ground pepper and/or herbs may be rubbed into it. Place the roast, fat side up, on a rack in a roasting pan, so the melting fat can baste the meat as it cooks. Test for doneness by inserting an instant-read thermometer into the center of the roast (but not touching bone). The temperature should be 125°F (52°C) for rare or 140°F (60°C) for medium-rare; the meat closer to the ends will be more well done, giving your guests a choice of the degree of doneness.

PORK

Trim off any excess fat (with ham, a layer of fat is left to garnish with cloves and to baste the meat). Rolled boneless roasts should be tied with kitchen string every 1½ inches (4 cm) or so to hold the roast closed and give it an even shape. Many pork recipes call for lightly sweet ingredients, such as fruit or Port, which complement the mild, sweet flavor of the meat. Test for doneness by inserting an instant-read thermometer into the thickest part of the meat (but not touching bone). Take care not to overcook pork, or it will be dry. Pork is considered safe to eat when the internal temperature reaches 160°F (71°C.) Already-cooked hams need only to be heated to 130°F (54°C).

LAMB

Trim off any excess fat and silver skin, a thin, silvery layer of membrane that is tough and can make meat curl. For a neat appearance and ease of carving, racks of lamb should be "frenched" by a butcher (see page 41). Check for doneness by inserting an instant-read thermometer into the thickest part of the meat (but not touching bone); the temperature should be 125°F (52°C) for rare or 135°F (57°C) for medium-rare.

CARVING

Before carving any roasted meat or poultry, let it rest (page 111). You may then carve the roast in the kitchen and serve it already sliced and attractively arranged in an over-lapping pattern on a platter or on individual plates. If you are confident of your skills, carve the roast at the table. Remember, your carving skills will improve with practice and using good-quality carving utensils will help make the process easier. Following are some tips to help you.

Use a two-pronged fork and a good-quality carving knife. A long, straight, serrated knife works well for sturdy meats like beef and ham. Some cooks prefer a slicing knife with a long, flexible blade for following the contours of a large turkey or goose. If you are using a knife that is not serrated, be sure to sharpen it well before each use. The best home tool to use is a sharpening, or butcher's, steel. Swipe each side of the cutting

edge a few times across and along the length of the steel, alternating sides and holding the blade at about a 15-degree angle. Also use a sturdy, slip-resistant carving board, preferably one with a narrow groove around the perimeter to capture escaping juices.

Rib roasts are carved by cutting through the meat between the ribs to serve each person a rib section. Boneless pieces of meat are carved by cutting the meat against the grain. This produces a more handsome slice. Ham is carved by cutting slices vertically down to the bone, beginning at the narrow end of the ham, then making a horizontal cut along the bone to release the slices. Cut three-fourths of the ham into slices and leave the slices on the ham to bring to the table for an attractive presentation. Brisket is sliced against the grain on a diagonal. To carve a rack of lamb, cut between the bones into individual chops. In all cases, use the carving fork to hold the meat steady while slicing the meat.

Most meats are cut into slices about ¼ inch (6 mm) thick, although very tender meats, such as a standing rib roast, may be cut a little thicker as they are easier to chew. When carving, do not change the direction of the knife blade in midslice, or the pieces will be ragged and uneven.

Carve only the meat that will be consumed at the meal. Leftovers will stay juicier if they remain uncarved. To carve poultry, begin on one side of the bird and completely carve this side before moving to the other. Shown opposite are the basic steps.

1 Remove the wings: With the bird breast side up, cut through the skin between the wing and breast. Pull the wing away from the body to locate the shoulder joint and cut through the joint to remove the wing.

2 Remove the whole legs: Cut through the skin between the thigh and body. Pull the leg away from the body and slice through the skin to locate the thigh joint. Cut through the joint to remove the entire leg.

3 Separate the thigh and drumstick: Cut through the joint that separates these two pieces. Serve the pieces whole, or carve them by cutting off the meat in thin slices parallel to the bone.

4 Carve the breast: At the bottom of one breast, just above the breastbone, make a horizontal cut through the breast toward the bone to create a base cut. Starting near the outside edge of the breast, carve thin diagonal slices, cutting downward to end each slice at the base cut.

DEGLAZING

Deglazing is a French technique that takes advantage of the browned bits on the bottom of a pan to make a flavorful sauce for meat and poultry. This step also helps to produce gravy that is rich, brown, and delicious.

To deglaze, remove the roast from the pan and remove as much of the excess fat from the drippings as you can. Pouring the drippings into a fat separator or large glass measuring pitcher will facilitate this process. The fat will rise to the surface and you can either pour it off or use a large spoon to skim it away. Some recipes may direct you simply to tilt the pan and spoon off the fat. To absorb the last bit of fat, briefly float a piece of paper towel on the surface of the drippings. Sometimes a portion of the removed fat is returned to the drippings to enrich the sauce or gravy. Put the remainder in a jar or can for discarding.

Set the pan over medium heat and pour in a small amount of stock, wine, or water. As the liquid simmers, stir with a wooden spoon to scrape up the browned bits from the bottom. Cook to reduce to a flavorful sauce and serve it over or alongside the meat. Or use it as the base for a sauce or gravy by adding other ingredients, such as cream or herbs.

FOOD SAFETY TIPS

Food safety is an important consideration during the holidays, a time when the refrigerator, table, and counters are crowded with food. To protect your family and guests, keep these precautions in mind:

Your refrigerator must be cold enough for safe storage. A refrigerator thermometer placed on the top shelf should read no higher than 40°F (4°C).

Make sure that raw meat is not leaking in your refrigerator. You may need to place the meat on a rimmed tray so that its juices won't drip onto and contaminate other food.

Let foods that are hot cool before putting them in the refrigerator; otherwise, they can lower the internal temperature of the refrigerator and compromise the safety of the other food stored there.

Before cooking, rinse poultry—turkey, goose, chicken—under cold running water, both flushing out the cavities and washing the outside well.

When handling raw meat, especially poultry, wash your hands thoroughly with warm water and lots of soap both before and after you work with the meat.

Rinse fruits and vegetables well under cold running water, scrubbing those that will not be peeled especially well to rid them of any pesticide residue. If the zest of a citrus fruit will be used, scrub it particularly well. Dunk leafy greens and lettuces in a large basin or sink filled with water to remove any pesticide residue and trapped grit and sand, changing the water as needed until it is clear.

Use separate cutting boards for animal products and for produce. Thoroughly wash any cutting surfaces, dishware, cookware, and kitchen tools that come in contact with the raw food.

Do not let raw meat or dairy foods sit at room temperature for more than 2 hours.

Never put stuffing into a turkey or other poultry the day before (or even several hours before) roasting. Raw poultry juices may introduce bacteria. Stuff the turkey just before putting it into the oven, and make sure to cook it until an instant-read thermometer inserted into the stuffing itself registers 160°F (71°C). Remove the stuffing from the bird completely before serving and transfer it to a serving bowl.

At the end of a meal, do not leave leftovers sitting out for more than 2 hours. Instead, cover or wrap well and refrigerate or freeze as soon as possible. Leftover turkey or other poultry should be removed from the bones before storing.

BASIC RECIPES

Here are some basic recipes referred to throughout this book.

CHICKEN STOCK

1½ lb (750 g) chicken parts, including backs, wings, necks, and any leftover bones from cooked chicken

1 small yellow onion, halved

1 carrot, peeled and cut into large chunks

1 celery stalk with leaves, cut into large chunks

1 bay leaf

5 peppercorns

3 fresh flat-leaf (Italian) parsley sprigs

Rinse the chicken parts under cold running water. In a large saucepan or stockpot, combine the chicken parts with the onion, carrot, celery, bay leaf, peppercorns, and parsley. Add 8 cups (64 fl oz/2 l) water. Bring to a boil over high heat. Reduce the heat to medium-low, and simmer, uncovered, until flavorful, about 45 minutes, skimming the foam from the surface occasionally.

Strain the stock through a fine-mesh sieve into a bowl. Discard the solids. Let cool, then cover and refrigerate overnight. Remove the congealed fat from the surface. Cover and refrigerate the stock for up to 3 days, or pour into airtight containers and freeze for up to 3 months. Makes about 7 cups (56 fl oz/1.75 l).

TURKEY STOCK

Neck and giblets (page 122) of 1 turkey

1 small yellow onion, halved

1 carrot, peeled and cut into large chunks

1 celery stalk with leaves, cut into large chunks

1 bay leaf

5 peppercorns

3 fresh flat-leaf (Italian) parsley sprigs

Rinse the neck and giblets. Reserve the liver for another use, such as poaching and then chopping to add to stuffing, dressing, or gravy.

In a saucepan, combine the turkey neck, gizzard, and heart with the onion, carrot, celery, bay leaf, peppercorns, and parsley. Add 4 cups (32 fl oz/1 l) water. Bring to a boil over high heat, reduce the heat to medium-low, cover partially, and simmer until flavorful, about 30 minutes, skimming the foam from the surface occasionally.

Strain the stock through a fine-mesh sieve. Discard the solids. Cover and refrigerate the stock for up to 3 days, or pour into airtight containers and freeze for up to 3 months. Makes about 3 cups (24 fl oz/750 ml).

SPONGE CAKE

5 large eggs, separated, at room temperature

¾ cup (6 oz/185 g) sugar

1 teaspoon vanilla extract (essence)

¼ teaspoon fine sea salt

1 cup (4 oz/125 g) cake (soft-wheat) flour

Preheat the oven to 350°F (180°C). Line the bottom of a 9-inch (23-cm) springform pan with a round of parchment (baking) paper or waxed paper. In a bowl, whisk the egg yolks and ½ cup (4 oz/125 g) of the sugar together until the mixture is pale and the batter is thick enough to leave a slowly dissolving ribbon on the surface when dropped from the whisk, about 4 minutes. Beat in the vanilla.

In a large bowl, using a balloon whisk, beat the egg whites until foamy. Add the salt and beat until soft peaks form. Beat in the remaining sugar a little at a time, until stiff, glossy peaks form. Stir a large spoonful of the whites into the yolk mixture to lighten in. Sift a third of the flour over the batter and gently fold it in until blended. Fold in half of the remaining whites. Sift another third of the flour over the batter and fold in. Repeat with the remaining whites and flour, ending with the flour.

Pour the batter into the prepared pan and smooth the top. Bake until golden brown and puffed, 35–40 minutes. Transfer the pan to a wire rack and let the cake cool for 10 minutes. Remove the sides of the pan. Invert the cake onto the rack and remove the pan bottom and the paper. Turn the cake right side up and let cool completely. Makes one 9-by-2-inch (23-by-5-cm) cake.

SUGGESTED MENUS

When choosing dishes to make up a Christmas or other holiday menu, choose foods that will contrast and harmonize with each other. Avoid courses that use the same ingredients or are the same colors and textures. Instead, try to balance these elements throughout the meal.

Here are five suggested menus using the recipes in this book; you will easily come up with your own custom-made ones. Don't forget the recipes in the Open House chapter!

AN ENGLISH CHRISTMAS DINNER

Oyster Stew with Fresh Rosemary

Standing Rib Roast with
Yorkshire Pudding

Roasted Root Vegetables with
Shallots and Thyme

English Trifle with Pears
and Dried Cherries

A NEW YEAR'S EVE DINNER

Butternut Squash and Apple Soup

Red Oakleaf and Frisée Salad
with Persimmons

Rack of Lamb with
Cranberry-Chile Relish

Mashed Potatoes and Celery Root

Chocolate Mousse Cake

AN OLD-FASHIONED CHRISTMAS DINNER

Crab Bisque

Watercress and Endive Salad with
Warm Bacon Vinaigrette

Roast Brined Turkey with Corn Bread
and Sausage Dressing

Creamed Spinach

Mashed Potatoes and Celery Root

Persimmon-Cranberry Pudding

A WINTER SOLSTICE FEAST

Spinach Salad with
Blood Oranges and Fennel

Roast Pork Loin Stuffed
with Dried Fruits

Gratinéed Leeks

Wild Rice Pilaf with
Dried Cranberries and Pecans

Ginger Cake with Orange Zabaglione

A HANUKKAH CELEBRATION

Red Oakleaf and Frisée Salad
with Persimmons

Brisket Braised in Red Wine

Latkes with Pear-Cherry Chutney

Baked Acorn Squash with
Maple Syrup and Balsamic Vinegar

Citrus Compote

GLOSSARY

BLACK WALNUTS Notoriously hard to crack but with a distinctive, rich flavor, black walnuts grow wild throughout much of the United States. If you don't have access to black walnut trees or don't have the time to crack the nuts, the nut meats are available from specialty-food shops and by mail order. Pecans also make a fine substitute.

CARDAMOM A tropical spice that is traditionally used in baking and in Indian cuisine, cardamom seeds are available already ground or still in the pods, which look like papery tan berries. Grinding your own is preferable, as the spice will be more flavorful. Split open the husks to release the seeds and grind them in a mortar or a spice grinder.

CAYENNE PEPPER When ground, dried red cayenne chiles yield a bright orange-red powder that adds spark to many dishes. Since it is a powerful spice, use a tiny amount at first and then increase it according to your taste.

CHERRIES, DRIED TART Unlike dried Bing cherries, sun-dried tart cherries contribute a sweet-tart flavor as well as color to winter dishes. Look for them in specialty-food shops.

CHIVES These brilliant green spears lend color and a mild onion flavor when minced and added to savory dishes. The minced green portions of green (spring) onions may be substituted.

COINTREAU An orange-flavored liqueur, Cointreau adds depth and flavor to drinks, desserts, and dessert sauces. Other orange liqueurs, such as Triple Sec or Grand Marnier, may be substituted.

CRÈME FRAÎCHE True French crème fraîche is made from matured unpasteurized cream; the natural fermentation gives it a faintly sour taste similar to that of sour cream. Crème fraîche adds a nutty tang to foods, and, unlike sour cream, it can be heated without curdling. It can also be whipped, like heavy (double) cream, though it won't mound as high. Look for crème fraîche in the dairy section of your market, or make your own: In a small saucepan, combine 1 cup (250 ml) heavy cream (not ultrapasteurized) and 2 teaspoons buttermilk. Heat over low heat just until lukewarm, 80°F (27°C). Pour into a bowl, cover loosely with plastic wrap, and let stand at room temperature until thickened, 8–24 hours, depending on the heat of the room. Stir, cover again, and refrigerate for up to 10 days.

CUMIN An ancient aromatic spice believed to be native to the eastern Mediterranean, cumin lends a nutty, smoky flavor to food. It is available already ground or as light brown, round seeds that can be toasted and ground.

DOUBLE BOILER Foods that must be heated or melted carefully to prevent scorching, such as egg yolks and chocolate, should be cooked over barely simmering water in a double boiler, a set of two nesting pans. In the absence of a double boiler, substitute a stainless-steel bowl over a saucepan of simmering water; make sure the bottom of the bowl does not touch the water.

EGG, RAW Eggs are sometimes used raw in eggnog and other preparations. Raw eggs run a risk of being infected with salmonella or other bacteria, which can lead to food poisoning. This risk is of most concern to small children, older people, pregnant women, and anyone with a compromised immune system. If you have health and safety concerns, do not consume raw egg.

FENNEL This vegetable is valued for its green-white bulb, feathery fronds, and pungent seeds. Fennel is at its best in winter, when the bulb adds its crisp texture and faintly sweet licorice flavor to salads. The bulbs can also be grilled or baked. To use, cut off the long hollow stems and any discolored areas from the bulb, saving the feathery fronds to snip with scissors or to use whole as a garnish.

FOLDING This technique is used to blend two mixtures (or ingredients) of different densities without losing volume or loft. To fold, spoon some of the lighter mixture into the heavier mixture and, using a rubber spatula, cut down through both of the mixtures to the bottom of the bowl. Using a circular motion, bring the spatula up along the side of the bowl farthest from you, lifting up some of the mixture from the bottom of the bowl and "folding" it over the top one. Rotate the bowl a quarter turn and repeat just until both have been blended.

FRISÉE Also called curly endive, this member of the chicory family is a pale yellow-green, with thin, spiraling fringed leaves. At its best during the cold months, it is typically combined in small amounts with other greens to provide a contrast in color and texture as well as its refreshingly bitter flavor.

GIBLETS The liver, heart, and gizzard of poultry, giblets are usually packaged inside the bird, along with the neck. Use the giblets and neck to make poultry stock, but cook the liver separately, as it can add a bitter taste to the other parts. Chop the liver to add to gravy or stuffing.

GINGER This knobby rhizome, or underground stem, adds spark and warmth to winter dishes; it is excellent to keep on hand year-round to mix with dried ginger in cakes and cookies. You can freeze the entire piece of ginger in a freezer bag and grate it, still frozen.

Or you can cut the piece into large chunks and submerge them in a glass jar of dry sherry, dry white wine, or dry white vermouth. Covered and refrigerated, the ginger will keep for several months.

MADEIRA A Portuguese fortified wine with a nutty, mellow flavor. Madeira enhances both sweet and savory dishes. It is also served before or after dinner with cheese and nuts.

MARSALA This Sicilian fortified wine is available either dry or sweet. Use the dry wine in preparing sweet and savory dishes or for serving as an aperitif; sweet Marsala may be used in desserts or poured as an after-dinner drink.

MUSHROOMS To clean mushrooms, gently brush them with a damp cloth or mushroom brush or other soft brush. This is preferable to rinsing them since mushrooms will soak up water like a sponge. Following is some information about the mushroom varieties used in this book.

Chanterelles: Found only in the wild, chanterelles look like long, golden trumpets with a fluted and fringed bell.

Cremini: Resembling domesticated white button mushrooms in shape and size, cremini are mottled brown in color. They have a firmer texture and fuller flavor than white mushrooms, making them good for cooking.

Porcini: Also known as ceps and king boletes, porcini are prized for their dense, meaty flesh and rich flavor. Fresh porcini are available in some markets only briefly in late spring or autumn, but dried porcini are found in many food stores.

Portobellos: When full grown, cremini become huge portobellos. These mushrooms can be as large as saucers, with dark brown gills and mottled brown caps.

White Buttons: Shaped like round buttons and domestically grown, these are the most commonly available mushrooms.

NONALUMINUM Uncoated aluminum or cast-iron pans can react with acidic ingredients, such as eggs or citrus juice, causing the food to discolor and develop an "off" flavor. When cooking with these ingredients, it is best to use cookware made of, or lined with, nonreactive substances, including stainless steel, enamel, or glass, or to use anodized aluminum cookware.

OIL, CANOLA A mild oil processed from the crushed seeds of rape, a member of the mustard family, canola oil is high in healthful monosaturated fat.

OIL, GRAPESEED This oil from the crushed seeds of grapes has a high smoking point and a mild flavor; it is high in healthful monosaturated fat.

PEPPER, WHITE White and black peppercorns start off as the same berries on the tropical pepper bush. Black peppercorns that are soaked to remove their skins become white peppercorns, which are prized by many cooks because they have a milder flavor and their pale color is more pleasing in light-colored foods.

PERSIMMONS See page 69.

RICER Ideal for preparing fluffy mashed potatoes and other purées, this utensil has a perforated container to hold cooked vegetables and fruits. When the ricer's handles are pressed together, the food is forced through the perforations, and any fibers or peels are left behind in the container.

RUM A liquor distilled from sugarcane, rum is available in light and dark versions. Dark rum is preferable in most desserts, as it has a fuller flavor.

SALT, KOSHER Kosher salt is preferred by many cooks because it has no additives and because its coarse grains are easy to pick up in the fingers to add to foods when cooking.

SALT, SEA Gathered from salt pans on the edge of the sea, this salt contains no additives and has a clean, natural taste. It comes in both fine and coarse grinds; fine sea salt is best for most cooking.

SUGAR, SUPERFINE Also known as caster sugar, this finely ground granulated sugar is often called for in drinks and other recipes in which it is important

that the sugar dissolve quickly. It is ideal for making candied citrus peel because the sugar will coat the peel evenly. To make your own superfine sugar, whirl granulated sugar in a blender or food processor for a few seconds.

THERMOMETER, INSTANT-READ For quick, accurate checks for doneness of meat and poultry, use an instant-read thermometer, which is inserted in the food and responds within seconds. Don't leave this type of thermometer in the food while it is cooking.

TURMERIC When dried and ground, this tropical root is an intense yellow-orange. It is used primarily for the rich golden color it imparts to dishes.

VERMOUTH A fortified wine flavored with various spices, herbs, and fruits, vermouth is available sweet and red, sweet and white, or dry and white. Dry white vermouth, an ingredient in the classic martini, is excellent for use in cooking. Keep a bottle in your pantry (it does not need refrigeration after opening) and use it in any recipe that calls for dry white wine. Vermouth is an especially good liquid for deglazing to make a pan sauce (see page 116).

VINEGAR Stock your pantry with a variety of vinegars. Their subtly different flavors enhance everything from salads and sauces to main courses.

Balsamic: See page 46.

Distilled White: Clear and sharp-flavored, distilled vinegar is made from grain alcohol. It is often used in pickling and sometimes in salad dressings.

Pear: This lightly sweet, fragrant vinegar is produced from white wine vinegar flavored with pears. Try it in subtly flavored and light-colored dishes.

Raspberry: Flowery and sweet, this red vinegar is made from white wine vinegar flavored and colored by the addition of raspberries. Use in salad dressings and other dishes to complement oranges, beets, raspberries, or strawberries.

Red Wine: Sharply acidic, red wine vinegar is produced when red wine is fermented for a second time. Blend into vinaigrettes for a full-bodied flavor.

Rice: Made from fermented rice, this delicate, lightly fragrant vinegar is especially good in mild-flavored dishes.

White Wine: Light in flavor and pale in color, this vinegar is produced from white wine. Use it in vinaigrettes and in savory dishes.

WATERCRESS A member of the mustard family, watercress grows wild in cold, shallow streams and along the edges of cold springs. Commercially, it is cultivated both in moist soil and hydroponically; in the latter case, it is sold with the roots intact and wrapped in cloth. It has a refreshing peppery flavor and brilliant green leaves, which add a bright note to winter salads.

INDEX

SIMON & SCHUSTER SOURCE
A Division of Simon & Schuster, Inc.
Rockefeller Center
1230 Avenue of the Americas
New York, NY 10020

WILLIAMS-SONOMA
Founder and Vice-Chairman: Chuck Williams

WELDON OWEN INC.
Chief Executive Officer: John Owen
President: Terry Newell
Chief Operating Officer: Larry Partington
Vice President, International Sales: Stuart Laurence
Creative Director: Gaye Allen
Associate Creative Director: Leslie Harrington
Series Editor: Sarah Putman Clegg
Editor: Heather Belt
Designer: Teri Gardiner
Production Director: Chris Hemesath
Color Manager: Teri Bell
Shipping and Production Coordinator: Libby Temple

Weldon Owen wishes to thank the following people for their generous assistance and support in producing this book: Copy Editor Kris Balloun; Consulting Editor Sharon Silva; Food Stylists Kim Konecny and Erin Quon; Photographer's Assistant Faiza Ali; Proofreaders Carrie Bradley and Arin Hailey; Production Designer Joan Olson; and Indexer Ken DellaPenta.

Williams-Sonoma Collection *Christmas* was conceived and produced by Weldon Owen Inc., 814 Montgomery Street, San Francisco, California 94133, in collaboration with Williams-Sonoma, 3250 Van Ness Avenue, San Francisco, California 94109.

A Weldon Owen Production
Copyright © 2003 by Weldon Owen Inc. and Williams-Sonoma Inc.

For information regarding special discounts for bulk purchases, please contact Simon & Schuster Special Sales at 1-800-456-6798 or business@simonandschuster.com

Set in Trajan, Utopia, and Vectora.

Color separations by Bright Arts Graphics Singapore (Pte.) Ltd.
Printed and bound in Singapore by Tien Wah Press (Pte.) Ltd.

First printed in 2003.

10 9 8 7 6 5 4

Library of Congress Cataloging-in-Publication Data

Miller, Carolyn.
 Christmas / recipes and text, Carolyn Miller ; general editor, Chuck Williams ; photographs, Maren Caruso.
 p. cm. — (Williams-Sonoma collection)
 At head of title: Williams-Sonoma.
 Includes index.
 1. Christmas cookery. I. Title: Williams-Sonoma Christmas. II. Williams, Chuck. III. Title. IV. Williams-Sonoma collection (New York, N.Y.)

TX739.2.C45M5497 2003
641.5'68—dc21

2003048335

ISBN 0-7432-5335-3

A NOTE ON WEIGHTS AND MEASURES

All recipes include customary U.S. and metric measurements. Metric conversions are based on a standard developed for these books and have been rounded off. Actual weights may vary.